ST ALBION
PARISH NEWS

BOOK 3

PREFACE BY THE VICAR

I never imagined that I would be writing a preface to another collection of my Parish Newsletters – but here I am!

And yet you know it makes a lot of sense when you think about it. I've been banging on about *the third way* in my sermons haven't I and now here's the *third book*!!

It's obviously not for me to judge whether it's better than the first or the second book but if it is as much of a success as the third *way* has been in St Albion's then it will be selling like Mr Sainsbury's GM-Free Hot Cakes at the Village Fête! (Good one, Alastair!)

You know, a lot of authors describe their books as their "babies" and when they publish a new one they talk as if they had just given birth!

Well, if I can be personal for a minute, I hope that this book will create a special bond between us – because when you buy it both you and I will be "holding the baby"! (Thanks Alastair for that one too!)

Yours paternally,

Published in Great Britain by
Private Eye Productions Ltd, 6 Carlisle Street, W1D 3BN.
© 2000 Pressdram Ltd
ISBN 1 901784 20 7
Designed by Bridget Tisdall
Printed in England by Ebenezer Baylis & Son Ltd, Worcester
2 4 6 8 10 9 7 5 3 1

SON OF BLAIR

THE SEQUEL

Further letters from the vicar,
the Rev. A.R.P. Blair MA (Oxon)

compiled for

PRIVATE EYE

by Ian Hislop, Richard Ingrams,
Christopher Booker and Barry Fantoni

Parish Personalities

No 1

Who says that the vicar takes all the limelight? Not us!
That's why we asked local artist Alan de la Nougerede
(11½) to make sketches of some of St Albion's
leading figures. And who better to start off with than
the editor of this newsletter?

A. Campbell, Spinster of this Parish

ST ALBION PARISH NEWS

17th September 1999

Hullo!

I am sure many of you will have been as saddened as I was to have seen on the news the tragic story of the 12-year-old girl, little more than a toddler, who has had a baby.

What kind of a society are we living in, where these things can happen?

What kind of a world is this where a young schoolgirl, with all her life ahead of her, is suddenly burdened with all the cares and woes of motherhood?

Isn't it every parent's worst nightmare?

These are the questions that I am sure we've all been asking ourselves.

And the answer, I'm afraid, is one that some of you aren't going to like very much.

It's about the "M-word". No, not money. There's nothing wrong with that, as Mr Sainsbury would be the first to remind us, after he put £2 million in the collection plate last week!

No, I'm talking about Morality. Something we don't talk about much now, do we?

But that's what this is all about. What we need is a new moral crusade, to make sure that the kind of things we see on our television screens (or read about on the internet!) never happen again.

We've got to build the kind of society where our children can enjoy their childhood and concentrate on getting 100 percent in their GCSEs, without worrying about which one of their boyfriends is the father of their baby.

"Easier said than done, vicar," I can already hear my friend from Tesco's saying to me.

Well, this is my answer to our friend, and all those Doubting Thomases (and Thomasinas!) who think that vicars are all talk and no action!

That's why we had a series of top-level talks at the vicarage to discuss what can be done about it. And this is what we've come up with.

1. *Proposed by Mr Straw, chairman of the St Albion's Neighbourhood Watch.*

An immediate curfew on all children in the parish, to ensure that they are all at home in bed (but not with each other, obviously!) after a certain time at night. We are still debating what that time should be, with options ranging from 4 o'clock in the afternoon, when school finishes, to 3 o'clock in the morning, when the St Albion's Youth Club XstasE closes down.

2. *Proposed by Mr Blunkett, chairman of the governors of the St Albion's Primary School.*

All children in the parish to be given lessons on the importance of marriage as a building block to a more cohesive society. The lectures will stress that although there are many equally valid lifestyle options, it would be foolish not to recognise the part marriage has to play in the society of the future.

Possible team-leaders for these lessons on "The Importance of Marriage" include Mr Robin Cook, Mr Chris Smith, Mr Nick Brown, Mr Mandelson and Mr Lairg (supported by his wife Mrs Dewar).

Anyone who has any other ideas about how to promote the great "Moral Crusade" should send them to Mr Campbell's live-in partner, who has kindly offered to help out on this one.

In the meantime, I have composed a new chorus – "We're All Going On A Moral Crusade" – to be sung to the tune of Sir Clifford Richard's great hymn Summer Holiday (We're all going on a).

We shall be trying it out at evensong this Sunday, so please learn the words before you come:

> *"We're all going on a moral crusade,*
> *No more sex for a week or two.*
> *We're all going on a moral crusade,*
> *So let's flush our drugs down the loo."*

(Words: Rev. A.R.P. Blair)

I think it could catch on!

Yours ever,

Tony

(Happily married to Mrs Cherie Booth – you should try it, Gordon!)

Millennium Tent Update

I am very pleased to be able to say that the St Albion's Millennium Tent is well on course for its opening in September 2000. An exciting new feature will be the "Antarium", a plastic replica of an ants' nest from Mr Sainsbury's allotment, containing well over 200 genuine ants. This will represent "The Virtues of Hard Work". The vicar is particularly keen on this exhibit, as he says "We can all learn a lot from the humble ants, as they go uncomplainingly about their duties, doing exactly what they are told by the leader ant (Antus antus blairus). That's the Latin for 'ant' for those of you, like Mr Prescott, who did not have the benefit of a proper education (no disrespect intended, John!)."

C. Falconer, Chairman of the St Albion's "Millennium Tent Experience"

ANNOUNCEMENT

Mr Cook would like to thank all of you who have taken part in parish alms-giving over the last year.

The alms have been greatly appreciated by the poor people of Indonesia.

In fact, Mr Cook says that they have got so many alms that we don't need to give them any more!

So, well done all!

As it says in the Good Book, "The Lion shall lie down with the Lamb, and the Hawk shall fly over and kill them both" *(Geneside, Chapter 4, vs. 11).*

MISSION NOT IMPOSSIBLE!

Our special thanks to local artist Geoff Thompson (7½) for sending in this charming study of the Vicar launching his Crusade.

ST ALBION PARISH NEWS

1st October 1999

Hullo!

And I hope you'll all forgive me if I take this opportunity to spell out once and for all my views on one of the most important issues confronting the human race today – fox-hunting.

Some older folk who live in the country seem to be very upset that I want to stop the hunt from meeting outside the vicarage.

Look, I'm not against hunting. I want to make that clear! But I am against hunting foxes. Nor am I against fishing. After all, Our Lord himself often went fishing, and even recruited fishermen to his team ministry. But you don't read about him recruiting any huntsmen in red coats, do you?

The Bible isn't full of men shouting tally-ho, as they inflict pain on innocent animals, is it?

Nor am I, in any sense, against shooting, so long as no one inflicts any suffering on the birds as they are blown humanely to pieces! I am sure that, if guns had been invented in the olden days, Peter would have saved a lot of trouble by shooting that cockerel before it crowed the third time.

I can already hear my friend from Tesco's asking me, in his clever dick way, "So, Vicar, is it alright to shoot fish? Or to fish for foxes?"

It is sad that the greatest moral debate of our time should be reduced to this nit-picking level. So, that's why I want to end all this silly argument, once and for all, before some of the more troublesome members of the congregation start parading around the vicarage with their banners, and their silly chants of "Tony is a phoney" (which, incidentally, isn't clever or funny, just because it rhymes!).

It's all quite simple.

Foxes have as much right to live as anyone else, except fish and birds. (And the other animals we eat, obviously!)

I hope that's clear!

Yours ever, Tony

P.S. Next week's newsletter will contain a full account of our annual parish outing, which this year, thank goodness, is in Bournemouth, where there are far fewer people eating bags of smelly chips and being sick on the pavement (no offence, Mr Prescott!).

Notices

● The **St Albion's Shooting Club** has registered a record membership this year. The Vicar would like to be the first to congratulate the club on its popularity. "May you succeed in all your aims!" he says.

● The **St Albion's Angling Club** has also registered a record membership. The Vicar would again like to congratulate them on this success. "I'm hooked!" he says.

Verses By A Local Poet (the Vicar!)

Every year I visit the
     Working Men's Club
Which is full of smoke and
     beer just like a pub
Although the old chaps are
     friendly and merry
I would rather be at home
     sipping a glass of sherry!

(This poem was recited by the Vicar during his annual visit to the Working Men's Club, where he was given a standing ovation. Unfortunately, he was not able to stay to hear it because he had to return to his parish duties. Many thanks to Mr Prescott for taking on the job of drinking pints and reminiscing all night about "the good old days"! T.B.)

Cherie meets some of this year's GCSE fashion students at their "show" in the Parish Hall. In the picture Alex is modelling a leather jacket from our local Oxfam shop and a trendy stick-on "beard" from World of Beards in the High Street.

MILLENNIUM TENT UPDATE

The first batch of tickets for the Tent went on sale in the Parish last week, and within hours the first one had been bought by Mrs C.B. She tells us, *"It will be a fantastic day out, and the kids will love it. Is that OK, Tony?"*

Meanwhile, preparations for all the exciting exhibits in the Tent are well under way. The art department of the St Albion's Primary School will soon be ready to unveil their life-size papier mâché model of a human figure. But don't think that's all there's going to be! On your day in the Tent, you will also be able to do the following amazing things:

- enjoy a real state-of-the-art "cuppa" in the Tea Experience Zone
- pit your wits against aliens in the Nintendo Game Zone
- imagine you are at the seaside in the Sandpit Experience Zone (supplied by World of Sand)
- watch an entire episode of Blackadder in the Old Videos Zone (supplied by Mr Murdoch's Adult Mags and Vids Emporium)
- leave your own personalised message (15 secs max) for people who will be alive in 2000 years' time in the Answerphone Zone
- watch how burgers and fries are made in the McDonald's Zone (and sample the end result for only £11.95!).

WATCH THIS SPACE
FOR MORE AND MORE "ZONES" AS THEY
COME ON LINE!

Condolences

I AM sure we would all like to send heartfelt sympathy (writes the Vicar) to the family of the very popular policeman, Inspector Morse, who has recently died, as some of you may have read in the Daily Telegraph. He was a fine officer and will be sorely missed by everyone in the parish. A memorial service will be arranged (date to be announced). Have I got this right, Alastair? T.B.

ST ALBION PARISH NEWS

15th October 1999

The Parish News is proud and privileged to be able to publish for the first time the full, abridged, authorised version of the historic sermon delivered by the Vicar to a rapt congregation of thousands at the Church of St Conference Centre, Bournemouth (and written by myself A.C.! Editor).

BROTHERS AND SISTERS!

It's marvellous to be here, and everyone is very welcome! Especially any foxes who want to join us!

No, but seriously, my text today is taken from that great reformer and modernist, St Martin Luther the King. "Set my people free." That's what he said. And isn't that, in a very real sense, what we at St Albion's are trying to do?

What do we want to be set free from? I will tell you. They're what I call "the three Ps"!

We want to be free from PREJUDICE!

We want to be free from PRIVILEGE!

We want to be free from the PAST!

The old days are gone! In St Albion's today anybody is free to join us in church and to help us in our work!

You don't have to be rich! (Though there's nothing wrong with being rich!)

You don't have to have a fancy title to your name! (Although many of our friends have one!)

You don't have to have a posh voice and a private education! (Though the fact that I have, and Mr Prescott doesn't, is a definite advantage!)

There's no difference nowadays between the classes. We don't have the Squire sitting in the front pew and the poor man standing at the back!

Today the front pew is reserved for anyone, from any background, who wants to give a large donation to the running of the church!

So, that's why it is important that we identify all those forces which are holding us back in our great mission.

You know, some people say they no longer believe in the devil! But we in this church know better.

We know that the devil is at work everywhere. The forces of devilism are constantly at work, trying to undermine everything I do!

If you want to know who the devil is, I'll tell you!

The devil is the grumpy old parishioner who sits at the back complaining about all the changes I'm making!

The devil is the man in Tesco's who thinks he knows better than I do!

The devil is the man in the Cool Britannia Arms who tries to make silly jokes at my expense!

The devil is anyone in the parish who does not believe with every fibre of his being that what I am trying to do is the only way, the one true way, the third way!

(Ovation)

Wasn't it Our Lord who said "I am the good shepherd, and you lot are just a load of useless sheep who should do what you are told" *(Book of St Tony the Divine, Ch. 12)*?

So, let us all stand and renounce the devil and all his works, in all his many disguises.

The devil in the cloth cap. The devil in hunting pink. The devil in ermine robes. The devil carrying a handbag.

The small, bald sixth-form devil who thinks he's so clever.

(Laughter and applause)

When I see all these devils trying to oppose me, I think of that great Victorian saint, St Oscar of Reading, who described them as "the unbearable in pursuit of the unbeatable (ie me)".

(Laughter)

Remember, you are all free! So, please feel free to stand up and applaud for as long as you like!

(HUGE OVATION LASTING FOR FIVE HOURS)

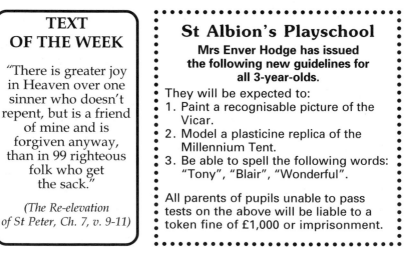

TEXT OF THE WEEK

"There is greater joy in Heaven over one sinner who doesn't repent, but is a friend of mine and is forgiven anyway, than in 99 righteous folk who get the sack."

(The Re-elevation of St Peter, Ch. 7, v. 9-11)

St Albion's Playschool

Mrs Enver Hodge has issued the following new guidelines for all 3-year-olds.

They will be expected to:
1. Paint a recognisable picture of the Vicar.
2. Model a plasticine replica of the Millennium Tent.
3. Be able to spell the following words: "Tony", "Blair", "Wonderful".

All parents of pupils unable to pass tests on the above will be liable to a token fine of £1,000 or imprisonment.

From the Postbag...

Dear Sir,

As an old-age parishioner who has been on every parish outing since 1928, I would like to say how disgusted I was at the dropping of the traditional hymn at the end of this year's outing: "There Is A Red Flag Far Away". Instead, we were all expected to sing a tuneless new song (no doubt written by the Vicar) which

> *Yours faithfully,*
> *Barbara Castle (Mrs),*
> *The Very Old Folks Home,*
> *Keir Hardie Close.*

The Editor reserves the right to cut all letters designed to embarrass the Vicar on the grounds that their authors are obviously in league with the devil. A.C.

PCC Notices

● Mr Cunningham has decided to step down as Churchwarden. This is a very sad day for all of us – but especially Jack because he wasn't up to the job and should have resigned ages ago. Our thoughts go with you.

● Mrs Mowlam has done such a good job running the St Albion Mission to St Gerry's in Northern Ireland that she is to come home at once and take over Mr Cunningham's job.

● Mr Dobson has decided that he is giving up his job running the St Albion's Cottage Hospital in order to devote his energies full-time to playing the part of Dick Whittington in the Millennium Pantomime. This may come as a surprise to Frank, but it is really what he wants most and will stop Mr Livingstone from making a fool of himself. The last time he played the Mayor of London he got all the lines wrong and tried to upstage the Vicar! And we don't want that, do we?

● My friend Mr Mandelson will take over from Mrs Mowlam due to overwhelming public demand (from myself) for his reappointment to the PCC!

X X X A BIG THANK YOU! X X X

The Vicar would like to thank everyone who worked so hard behind the scenes to make our Bournemouth outing such a triumph.

In particular, we all owe a great debt of gratitude to **Mr Marks** and **Mr Gran** of the Birds Of A Feather Joke and Novelty Shop in the High Street for supplying such excellent "gags" to liven up the Vicar's speech. It's not giving away any trade secrets to reveal that the joke about "What a stupid hunt" was theirs!

Many thanks to **Mr Sainsbury** for his generous contribution to the harvest festival. He filled the entire nave with one tomato which smelt marvellously of haddock! We are sending it to East Timor as a harvest gift. T.B.

ST ALBION PARISH NEWS

29th October 1999

Hullo!

The year is changing. And what a positive thing that is!

Even nature realises that we've all got to move on. I mean, there may be some leaves that want to stay on the tree. But even the oldest, brownest and most shrivelled-up leaf must eventually be blown off in the winds of change. (Mr Benn will know who I am talking about!)

Everywhere we look, we find the same sad evidence of resistance to change, by people who don't realise that it's nature's way (the third way!).

In our schools, in our hospitals, and even in the church itself, there are those who want to keep things as they are.

They are scared of change. But are the trees scared of change? Are the birds scared of change, when they fly off in the winter to find better living standards for themselves and their families?

Do the squirrels complain that it is not summer any more, as they store up prudent stocks of nuts for the winter?

No! All God's creatures agree with me that change is nature's way to make things better.

We've all recently been watching those dinosaurs on the television.

And what a message they send to us all today, 893 million years later!

You have to change! Or sooner or later you will become extinct!

So, I've written a little chorus for all you teachersauruses and doctorsauruses:

"Change, change, change,
And here's the reason why.
'Cos if you don't keep changing,
Like the dinosaurs, you'll die!"
(Words and music by A.R.P. Blair)

Let's try this at our joint-benefice evensong on Sunday, shall we?
Your friend,

Tony

PS. Talking of change, I was stopped by a young man by the cashpoint in the High Street the other day, asking me "Have you got any change, Vicar?" "You bet," I said, "but I'm not giving you any. I'm talking about real change, change to bring about a better world. That's the only change you're going to get out of me!" And do you know, he went away looking very impressed!

BAD MANNERS TO AN HONOURED GUEST

THE VICAR WRITES:

I would like to put on record my extreme displeasure at the behaviour of those who tried to interrupt our visiting preacher, Mr Zemin, of the Chinese Atheists Society. It was the height of bad manners to shout silly slogans and wave flags while our distinguished visitor was being shown round the parish. We are all very concerned about China's problems, but there is a time and a place to discuss these things, and it is not when he is here as our guest. I am glad to say that the culprits have been identified and arrested. T.B.

● *The latest in Mr Cook's Modern Ethics series entitled 'Pinochet – why we must stand up to murderous dictators' has been postponed out of courtesy to Mr Zemin and has been rescheduled to take place after Mr Zemin has left the country.*

That's what I call good manners, Robin! Thanks! T.B.

✂

VOTING SLIP FOR THE ELECTION OF LORD MAYOR OF LONDON

The Vicar has decided that it should be up to you, the parishioners, to decide who gets the important role of Mayor of London in the St Albion's pantomime. So, please just fill in the form below and indicate who you want. This is a democratic parish, so let's not hear any more nonsense about the Vicar trying to fix things. **Simply tick the appropriate box.**

☐   Yes, I want nice Mr Dobson to be Mayor.

☐   No, I don't want Mr Livingstone under any circumstances.

PARABLES FOR THE NEW MILLENNIUM

The Prodigal Friend

THERE was once a very good man who had two friends, one called Peter and the other Geoffrey. And Peter got into a bit of trouble, living beyond his means in the fleshpots of Notting Hill. And Geoffrey helped Peter in his spendthrift ways by giving him an enormous cheque for a million talents (roughly £373,000 in today's money). And the good, wise and saintly man was furious that his friends were caught out borrowing and lending money in this wise, and he cast them both into outer darkness.

And for ten months Peter and Geoffrey lived in the wilderness. But one day Peter reappeared and said to his friend, "Tony, I am a changed man. I have paid back to Geoffrey all the money which he lent me, even every penny. And I am proud to say that I have become very humble. Now can I have my job back?" And his friend was overjoyed at the return of the prodigal, and welcomed him with open arms.

But then his other friend Geoffrey reappeared, saying "Can I have my job back also? For I have also lent money to you." But the wise, great and saintly man said unto him, "I have no idea what you are talking about. If you repeat any of it in public, you will be arrested."

Notices

There will be a special half-day session on the Internet in the Parish Hall on Friday afternoon which the vicar will be attending personally. He suggests that all parishoners do the same. "This is the future," he says. "This is the Information Super-Third-Way!"

ST ALBION PARISH NEWS

12th November 1999

Bonjour!

That's the French for "hullo"! And if you're wondering why I am addressing you in this way, it's because I'm getting pretty sick and tired of all this silliness that's been going on in the parish recently!

I was in Tesco's over the weekend and I was shocked to see a notice over the meat counter reading "Buy British And Tell The French To Frog Off!"

And that wasn't the worst of it. As I walked past the fruit counter, a group of elderly ladies were hurling French Golden Delicious apples into the street, shouting "Hands off our Coxes".

And, do you know, I had to say to these ladies: "Ladies, do try and control yourselves. You won't get your way in this world by throwing food around and shouting childish slogans about your neighbours.

"You should remember what Our Lord said. He said we should love our neighbours, not throw their food into the street" *(Gospel According to St Mark and St Spencer).*

And how right I was proved! Only ten days later, after I and my French colleague Father Jospin had talked things through in a proper Christian spirit of give and take, a thoroughly sensible agreement was reached which solved the whole problem.

Father Jospin explained how he would love to serve British beef at his church barbecue, but that some of his parishioners had threatened to burn down the church if such a thing was allowed.

I agreed that this was perfectly reasonable, and that as a reciprocal gesture, we would serve French beefburgers at our fireworks party.

So everyone was happy and it was all done without anyone throwing their weight around or getting angry, except of course our friend Mr Brown who made a bit of an idiot of himself by saying that he personally would boycott the Communion wine because it came from France.

Mr Brown has now written me a full apology for his very silly and annoying behaviour, in exchange for which I agreed not to mention the matter in the parish newsletter.

So, let that be an end to it, and let's turn our minds to more important matters, like making sure that Mr Dobson is chosen to play the part of Lord Mayor of London in the St Albion's pantomime.

Yours ever,

Tony

Notices

■ The St Albion Hunt will definitely meet outside the vicarage on 20 November as planned, although it may not if I am wet. T.B.

■ Videos of the Vicar's recent controversial sermon on "The Forces Of Conservatism" are no longer available. I would be grateful if no one asked for it again. A.C.

■ Mr Robinson will not be showing his supposedly controversial photographs in the village hall next week, or indeed at any other time, and if he tries he will be arrested. T.B.

 Parish Postbag...

Dear Sir,

My attention has been drawn to a number of highly defamatory statements which have recently been disseminated in the parish by Mrs Janet Richard, the wife of Mr Richard (recently sacked member of the Parish Council). It has in particular been alleged that our client, ie myself, was on many occasions inebriated and that our client behaved like a school bully, particularly towards Mr Dewar, whose wife he had run off with. I have to say that these allegations constitute one of the greatest and most offensive libels that have ever been perpetrated against a senior and respected friend of the Vicar. We await your reply with interest (5.3 percent).

> *Lairg and Lairg,*
> *the Lairgover Suite,*
> *Pugin House (formerly*
> *the Parish Hall).*

P.S. It is also wholly without foundation that our client paid for the lavish refurbishment of his office suite out of monies accruing from the parish poor box. On the contrary, the decision to expand parish funds in this way was taken by the previous incumbent and it was a mere oversight that the order for my wallpaper was signed three days after I came into office.

The vicar's wife joins in prayers at the Festival of Diwallet as a guest of the Hinduja brothers – the very same brothers who have given so generously to our Millennium Tent

SECTION OF MR LAIRG'S WALLPAPER

£ £ £ £ £

£ £ £ £ £

£ £ £ £ £

£ £ £ £ £

£ £ £ £ £

Isn't it tasteful? T.B.

A Statement From The Matron Of The St Albion's Old People's Home, Mrs Jay

I am glad to report that our programme of modernising the home for distressed gentlefolk is proceeding very satisfactorily, even though one or two of the former residents have taken their eviction very badly. I am thinking in particular of Mr Burford who jumped up and down on the settee, shouting and screaming, and had to be sedated by the male nurses. But most of the old folk, I am glad to say, have co-operated by filling in the forms explaining why they wanted to stay on. Indeed, some of them have already been allowed back in, so long as they behave themselves and do exactly what they are told by me and the Vicar.

I would like to mention in particular Mr Snowdon, who has done so much good work for unmarried mothers.

Mrs M. Jay.

(Well done, Margaret! As the daughter of one of our previous incumbents, you've certainly proved that ability can be inherited! T.B.)

✠ To Remember In Your Prayers

● Mrs Janet Richard, who is suffering distress and depression after the unfortunate dismissal of her husband from the PCC for being no good at his job. Help her to remember that it is not helpful to go around the parish telling a pack of shameless lies about the Vicar and his legal adviser, Mr Lairg. Let her remember how lucky she is that Mr Lairg is a broad-minded and forgiving christian gentleman, who realises that Janet's unfortunate recent outbursts have been no more than a cry for help from a deranged and psychotic woman who needs to spend a long period of rest and silence in a closed order of nuns. T.B.

ST ALBION PARISH NEWS

26th November 1999

Hullo!

I know we don't hear much these days about the word "excommunication". But that doesn't mean to say that it has no place in a modern church. Because it does.

It's not just something we read about in boring old history books. It's something that's very relevant in the world of today.

Because what it's really about is loyalty. As Our Lord himself said, "He who is not for me, is a bastard" (*Gospel according to St John the Major, 3.7*).

When you sign on to become a member of the Church, you sign on to the whole package. You can't have people picking and choosing which bits they want to believe in, and which they don't. Goodness me! Where do you think the Church would be, if it allowed people just to believe whatever suits them at any given time?

What sort of Vicar would I be, if I said one thing one Sunday and then did a complete u-turn the next?

Our friend at the Tesco check-out counter wouldn't let me get away with that, would he? If, for example, I preached a sermon saying that foxhunting was immoral and should be banned as soon as possible, and then the next day said that perhaps it wasn't so bad after all!

Or if, as another example, I was to say that no one should ever be allowed to build houses on the field behind the vicarage, and then promptly sold the field to some developers, just because they'd given money to parish funds!

Well, you can imagine what a field day my critics would have if I behaved like that!

Which all brings me to the nub of what I want to talk about this week. As you all know, Mr Livingstone has recently been saying a lot of very silly things. Firstly, he has said that he can't accept some of the articles of faith, as laid down in the Book of Common Blair (1997 version).

Secondly, he has been going around questioning my judgement as vicar. And that, not to beat about the bush, is what amounts to another old-fashioned word, "heresy".

Now don't get me wrong. I don't want to see Mr Livingstone burned at the stake, or anything like that (although there are times,

I must admit, when I wouldn't mind!), but, frankly, the Church can't afford to have Mr Livingstone as a full member, if he won't toe the line and accept everything that is laid down in the Nice One Creed.

We all remember how it goes: "I believe in three ways..." etc.

But that's not good enough for Mr Livingstone. No. He wants to court cheap popularity by saying things that people want to hear, and going round smiling at everyone and getting his picture in the local paper.

Well, I could easily do that, if I wanted to. I could go round smiling at everyone and having my picture in the paper and getting my wife to dress up in fancy outfits.

But I've got better things to do. I've got a parish to run, which means I've got to take tough decision. Not just sit about making jokes to people in pubs in a silly voice. And the most important decision I have to make is whether to excommunicate Mr Livingstone. You have been warned, Ken!

Yours infallibly,

His Holiness,

TONE THE FIRST

A PERSONAL NOTE

I know this is the sort of thing she would hate, but I would like to put on record my appreciation of the wonderful job Cherie is doing as the parish's "First Lady". She always looks marvellous, and she never complains, however much it is costing her to buy all those lovely clothes that you like to see her in. The last thing Cherie would want you to know is that she pays for all those dresses out of her own pocket, which she can ill afford to do. And let me tell you, they do not come cheap, especially if you have to order them specially from places like New York and Milan! There was certainly no suggestion on Cherie's behalf that the parish should subsidise her wardrobe from the collection plate, although I personally think that's a good idea, although Cherie would have a fit if I said so in public! T.B.

Sun-Day!

This Sunday there will be a special thanksgiving service to celebrate 30 years of the Sun newspaper.

We all owe an enormous debt of gratitude to this unique newspaper which has done so much to brighten up all our lives. Some people might find the famous "Page Three" girls offensive. Or its lack of regard for the truth obnoxious. I know I do. But it would be unhelpful for me to say so, in case they start attacking me and asking for someone else to be the vicar.

Let's remember that wonderful quote by Vidal Sassoon, the famous World War One poet:

"At the dumbing down of the Sun and the rising of the circulation, we will remember it."

How very true that is! T.B.

The SUN shines on the Vicar!

👍 *CONGRATULATIONS...*

...to Peter Mandelson, head of the St Albion's Mission to St Gerry's. After only two weeks in the job, he has "banged heads together" and produced a miraculous result! As the Good Book says, "Blessed are the dealmakers, for they shall make deals" *(Book of Trimble)*. I knew it was a good idea to get our former Churchwarden back into the team ministry, and haven't I been proved right!

UNTO US A CHILD IS BORN

From the Editor

OUR warmest congratulations to Tony and Cherie who have been blessed with joyous news. It's a baby for the Millennium and I know that you will join with me in suggesting to Tony that we replace the traditional, old-fashioned Christmas service with a new "Blairmas" service to celebrate these new glad tidings! Rejoice!!

Alastair Campbell

Hullo!

Firstly, Cherie and I would like to thank literally everyone in the parish for the thousands of letters, cards and flowers which have been pouring into the vicarage ever since the great news that we are going to have a Millennium baby!

Nothing brings people together more than the arrival of a new baby, as we are particularly aware at this time of the year!

Even people one wouldn't have expected have been kind enough to pop round to offer their good wishes. Like young Master Hague who, I am sure, one day will be old enough to have a baby of his own, rather than just looking like one (and acting like one!).

There's nothing like becoming a father to make a man a more mature and responsible individual! I don't want to sound pompous, but there must be a message there for Mr Brown! (I mean Gordon, not Nick obviously!)

But enough of the baby, even if it is the most important thing that's happened in the parish for a long time! I am sure you will all be pleased to hear that Cherie is absolutely blooming, and has even been out dancing with some of her friends in the amateur theatrical community – apparently, the newly refurbished Operatic Society function room above Boots in the High Street is looking marvellous! (Such a pity that the production of the Mikado had to be cancelled because Mr Smith and his partner hadn't finished making the curtains in time!)

Anyway, enough of Cherie and the baby, suffice it to say that everyone is very pleased about the Happy Event, and looking forward to our special service of Thanksgiving on December 25.

Please learn the following carols which the choir is already practising for that big occasion: Cherie's Boy (or Girl) Child; God Rest Ye Cherie; Ding Dong Cherily On High; and many other traditional favourites (suitably adapted for the occasion, words and music T. Blair!).

But I mustn't go on about the baby, because I know it's not fair to those who, unlike Cherie and myself, have not been lucky enough to have what in the olden days they used to call "a blessing", but what we now, in our more enlightened era, call an "unplanned conception event"!

We have to remember that many people in our society have to live for personal reasons on their own: like Mr Brown or Mr Kennedy, the new pastor of the United Liberal Methodists. Or even Mr Livingstone, who has only his newts to console him when he comes home from the office (no offence, Ken, but frankly you can't dandle a baby newt on your knee, or be pictured kissing it on the front page of the local paper!).

I don't want in any way to sound smug over the fact that I am still capable of fathering a fourth child, when there are men a lot younger than me who seem to be incapable of having a first child, let alone a fourth! I am thinking of poor Master Hague (although, to look at him, you might think he is an old man, as he has lost all his hair and talks in a funny voice!).

I mustn't obviously devote the whole of this letter to the subject of the baby, but there is just one matter on which I would like to put everyone's mind at rest.

"How on earth will you cope, Vicar," everyone is asking "with all those sleepless nights?"

Look, my answer is that it won't make the slightest difference. I am up half the night anyway working to make St Albion's a better place for you all to live in. And sometimes I'm up all night sorting out the mess made by some of my colleagues on the PCC (see accompanying letter!).

But I'm not complaining! After all, that's why I'm the vicar! As the old phrase has it (and never was it more apt!): "It's my baby"! (And I promise that's the last time in this newsletter I mention that particular word!)

Yours,

Parish Postbag

Dear Vicar,

I was outraged to learn that behind our backs you were negotiating an ecumenical merger with the Church of the United Reformed Liberal Democrats, under their minister, the Rev. Ashdown. Those of us who remember the battles some of us have fought over the years to preserve the true faith, find the suggestion that

> *Yours faithfully,*
> *T. Benn, Typhoo Ho.*
> *Mazzawattee Estate,*
> *Brooke Bond Road,*
> *PG TIPS.*

The Editor reserves the right to shorten all letters due to reasons of space. A.C.

Meetings

■ **Cherie's talk to the Women's Institute on "Sensible Family Planning" has been postponed until further notice. A.C.**

ST GERRY'S MISSION TO IRELAND

A Message from Mr Mandelson

■ My heartfelt congratulations to all those who have been responsible for helping me to solve the Irish question in such a short time. When I took over from Mo, let's be honest, things were in a bit of a mess. Mr Trimble wasn't even talking to her (and who can blame him, quite honestly! Sometimes these things need a man's touch!) But now everyone is working together towards one goal, and a very seasonal one it is too – ie, peace on Earth and particularly in Northern Ireland! But there is one person who must take the credit for this brilliant breakthrough. Not me – but the man who had the courage and the foresight to appoint me to the job! P.M.

Thanks, Peter, for a very moving tribute. It's wonderful to have you back in the team! T.B.

A Statement From Mr Prescott, Hon Secretary of the St Albion's Working Men's Club and PCC Transport Co-ordinator

Dear Everyone (Comrades),

I am getting heartily tired and sick of the constant sneering and sniping coming from certain quarters close to the vicarage (not to mention everybody else) about me making a pig's ear of the arrangements for car parking, cycle paths and bus lanes in and around the church, which is totally untrue, since I have started a number of important initiatives with regard to all of the above matters in pursuivance of my integranted strategy of getting the parish up and running on all four wheels, which is not to say that there are not problems of a problematic kind but my job would be made considerably bloody easier if I could rely on the support

> Yours sincerely,
> J. Prescott,
> Working Men's Club.

(Mr Prescott's statement had to be very considerably cut on the grounds of space and general incoherence. I regret this. A.C.)

The Vicar replies:

I was very saddened to read John's heartfelt apology for the way he has recently been messing up his responsibilities on all fronts – according to his critics, that is! I think he is being too hard on himself. We all make mistakes from time to time. I may even have made some myself, in appointing certain people to jobs which are above their abilities: something one might be prone to do through feeling sorry for someone who hasn't had one's advantages in life, such as a good education and an ability to string two words together without making a fool of himself! T.B.

ST ALBION PARISH NEWS

24th December 1999

Hullo!

As this is the last time I will be able to address you all before the next Millennium, let me begin by wishing you all a "Happy New Thousand Years!"

Aren't we all lucky, actually, to be living today, at this tremendously important turning point in human history!

I know I am. When I think of all the possibilities that are opening up before us here at St Albion's, I feel very humble. Possibly more humble than anyone else feels, because I am lucky enough to be the "man in charge" at this pivotal node in our parish history (not to mention that of the rest of the world!).

As it says in the New Labour Bible: "Behold, I shall make all things new" *(Book of Exclusive Revelations, 16.3)*. And that's the whole point of the message, actually, that I'm trying to get across.

Let me give you an example. Just before Christmas I had the privilege of an early glimpse of our "Millennium Tent", that for months has been going up on the wasteground where the gas works used to be.

And, my goodness, what an amazing sight it was! Everyone was working flat out to make sure that everything would be ready for our special "Secular Thanksgiving Service Event" on New Year's Eve.

The Brownies, the Scouts, the Women's Institute and the staff of Mr Murdoch's Adult Vids and Mags Company were all beavering away like mad!

I wish I could name all the people whose efforts have gone into making the Tent such an enormous success even before it's opened but there isn't room in such a short letter!

I didn't have time to look round all the attractions, actually, but I did have time to pose for a photograph next to the giant four-foot plaster-of-paris model of a dinosaur made by the Reception class of the St Albion's Primary School! As I keep saying to you – haven't we all got something to learn from the fate of those dinosaurs, who failed to move with the times and were wiped out by a comet (quite rightly!)?

And what an array of amazing exhibits have been put together by enterprising members of the parish! Everything on display, actually, conveys the excitement of the future, not the cobweb-ridden past!

I am thinking, for instance, of the amazing "organic mouse-mat" made from recycled egg boxes that is the star exhibit of the Tent's "Technology Zone" (thanks to the Science Department of the St Albion's Comprehensive Grammar School!); or the large pile of ten pence coins in the "Faith Zone". Impressed? And I only wish the critics had been there when I visited the "Nutrition Zone" and was able to taste the "Millenniburger", which is five layers high, and comes courtesy of our local caterer Mr Ronald McDonald, at an amazing bargain price of only £19.99!

Perhaps then all the parish cynics would have had to eat their words (which would have been a lot less pleasant than one of Mr McDonald's delicious burgers, I can tell you!).

Isn't it a pity that when anything new is planned, there are always people who can only stand on the sidelines and sneer?

Their lack of vision over the Tent is symptomatic, actually, of their attitude to St Albion's as a whole.

Why can't they just show a bit of enthusiasm for a change, and admit that what we have achieved since I arrived two years ago is little short of a miracle!

Still, I don't want to end this Millennium Message on a negative note by saying how irritating I find all those who can think of nothing better to do than be critical of other people!

Yours, actually,

Tony

PS. I would just like to remind parishioners that although the Tent has been sold out for months, there are still plenty of tickets available. Ring Mr Falconer on his mobile 'phone: 0898 2000 2000.

Notices
CHRISTMAS COLLECTION

 It has been decided by the PCC that there will be no collection for the poor and homeless this year. Our parish "focus groups" have reported back that simply handing out money and food does nothing to solve our long-term aim of eradicating poverty for ever. (*"The poor will not always be with you,"* as it says in the Book of Ruthlessness!) T.B.

✝ To Remember In Your Prayers

● Mrs Mowlam, who has been having a bad time since her husband was sacked from his job, and she sadly lost her own job as leader of the Mission to St Gerry's. Let Mo remember that we all have to adapt to changing circumstances in life; and help her to understand that you can't just expect to go round asking Mr Murdoch for a lot of money in exchange for some tittle-tattle about the Vicar. May she remember the story of Judas Iscariot, who, despite being one of Our Lord's team, took a bribe in return for 30 pieces of silver (£350,000 in today's money). And look what happened to him! T.B.

Parish Postbag

Dear Sir,

For months the Vicar has been preaching to us that we should "turn the other cheek" when the French do the dirty on us. Many of us farmers in the parish will be bankrupt this Christmas thanks to that attitude. How about putting some backbone in the Vicar, not just

> *Yours sincerely,*
> *F. Giles,*
> *C/o NatWest Bank,*
> *The High Street.*

The Editor reserves the right to cut all letters for reasons of space. A.C.

Thank You...

...all for your lovely Christmas cards cards. I think the one I like best is this one, showing Peter with his new baby!

But do remember, Peter, "a dog is for life, unlike your job!" T.B.

ST ALBION PARISH NEWS

14th January 2000

Hullo! And a Happy New Millennium to you all!
Wasn't it fantastic? What a night! Everyone I've spoken to
agrees with me that our Millennium Tent celebration was the most
exciting thing that had ever happened to St Albion's!

From start to finish it was a total triumph! And when, on the
stroke of midnight, the Massed Choirs of the Cubs and Brownies lit
their Millennium sparklers and sang "Away In A Manger" to the
tune of John Lennon's "Imagine", I don't mind admitting that
Cherie and I both shed a tear!

But it's unfair to single out just that moment! There was so much
about our Millennium Evening that was unforgettable!

The Weightwatchers' Ladies Line Dance ensemble (those who
hadn't gone down with the flu!) were amazing, performing to a
selection of James Bond theme-tunes!

Wasn't Mr Fry from the Jokes 'n' Novelties Shop a hoot, with
his amusing monologue? (Though some of it was a bit risqué –
come on, Stephen, it's not clever or funny, that toilet stuff!)

And congratulations to Mr Wilmot from Stilts R Us for
entertaining us all so royally before he fell over. (You'll be pleased
to hear that he's making a full recovery in the Orthopaedic Unit of
St Albion's Cottage Hospital!)

And the "Zones" themselves were truly out of this world – the
"Body Zone" with its amazing 4 ft. high papier mâché model of a
human being (which was very nearly finished in time for the
opening!); the "Technology Zone" with its selection of computer
games, such as Zombiekiller III, Cybermurder and Nintendo
Badminton; the "Nutrition Zone" with its interactive burger-stand
(the kids loved this one! You just give the staff a £10 note, and they
give you a shake of your choice, fries and a Millenniburger!); and,
of course, we mustn't forget the "Multi-Faith Zone", with its
message of hope for the future symbolised by a single bare light-
bulb and a "prayer chair" for interdenominational meditation
(kindly lent by St Albion's Primary School).

All of which puts into perspective the so-called "hiccups" which
some people in the parish have been trying to blow up out of all
proportion.

Yes, it is true that a small minority of parishioners, not more
than a few thousand, failed to get their tickets on time, due to the

fact that Mrs Page had forgotten to send them out (goodness me, Jennie can't be expected to do everything!).

Yes, there were a few queues for some of the more popular exhibits – but that just goes to show how popular they were, doesn't it!

Yes, there was a separate entrance to the Tent for the Vicar's party, after our drinks in the vicarage – but that was for security, as advised by Mr Straw, the head of our Neighbourhood Watch, in case a stray firework landed on the Vicar's head and ruined the evening for everyone!

Yes, the much-looked-forward-to "Paddling Pool of Fire" was a bit of a disappointment, but Mr Falconer assures me that, if only the lights had been turned off, we would all have seen it clearly for a few seconds.

But to pretend that these tiny glitches amounted to a "total fiasco", as some people have said, beggars belief!

As I said in my Millennium Sermon, "The Tent is a beacon, lighting the way to the future, just as St Albion's itself is a beacon, shining out against all the forces of darkness-ism. That is why we must all be beacons, spreading the message of a new dawn as we enter a new era."

I have tried to put this message into a chorus which we will try out at our family service on Sunday:

> "New, new, new,
> > It's new for me and you.
> Old, old, old,
> > It's what we don't want to be told.
> New, new, new,
> > Is the song we all must sing.
> Old, old, old,
> > That is not the thing."

> Words and music, T. Blair.

Try and memorise the words, so that you don't just stand there on Sunday looking glum (like some people did at the Millennium Tent during Auld Lang Syne!).

Yours millennially!

Tony

✝ To Remember In Your Prayers

● Mr Dyke from the TV rental shop (and one of our sponsors) who I'm afraid lost his temper in the queue to get into the Millennium Tent. May Greg remember that anger is one of the Seven Deadly Sins, and as a lesson in humility it did him no harm at all to be kept waiting for a few hours out in the rain with all the ordinary parishioners. Remember, as it says in the New Labour Bible, "The last shall be last, and the first shall be first-class." (*Letter to the Millennians*)

● Mr Dobson, who wants to be the Lord Mayor in the pantomime but keeps laughing at all the wrong moments. May Frank remember that it's all very well being jolly but sometimes seriousness is required, and Ms Jackson — who also wants to be Mayor — is *very* good at being serious. Know what I mean, Frank?

● Mr Brown, who has done nothing wrong in buying a knock-down flat from a discredited local businessman who used to be a friend of mine but is now an ex-friend. Gordon will need all our support at this time of crisis and I for one certainly don't find his problems at all funny. Ha ha ha! T.B.

Notices

There will be no further joint services with the United Reformed Liberal Democrat Church. This is because their new minister, the Rev. Charles Kennedy, has failed to appreciate that the co-operation between our two churches could only work so long as there is a proper spirit of give and take: *I give the services, and Mr Kennedy will take round the plate.*

**LAYING ON OF HANDS
The Vicar heals a young
flu victim. A.C.**

1000 Days Of Tony!

Tony doesn't like any fuss about all his achievements, but he has allowed us to include this new portrait of him by local artist Mr Kent. And doesn't he look perfect? Humble enough to know that even though he has done a fantastic job to date, there is still more brilliant work for him to do. A.C.

ST ALBION PARISH NEWS

28th January 2000

Hullo!

And first this week, can I clear up a misunderstanding of what I said in my sermon at the early service last Sunday?

Some of you seemed to think that I had made a firm promise that all our collection money was going to be given to the St Albion's Cottage Hospital, to cope with the 'flu epidemic.

Look. I've got my notes in front of me as I write, and what I said was "It would be nice if we were to give all our money to help the sick."

And that's a very different thing, isn't it?

Of course, we'd all LIKE to give lots more money to the ministry of healing.

We'd LIKE give money to all sorts of good causes. To our old people. To our young people. To extending our church car park.

But, as it says in the Bible, "We have to live in the real world" (*The Book of Gordon*, 7.3).

That's not to say that we're not going to give lots of money to the cottage hospital. Of course we are!

We know there's a problem. It was a problem that was left to us by the previous incumbent, the Rev. Major.

I don't want to blame him, because it's too easy to blame other people for one's own failings. No one knows this better than Mr Milburn, who should have foreseen this 'flu epidemic and done something about it before it happened!

But that's all in the past. And we don't want to dwell too much on the past, do we?

So, that's why I am giving you my word that our cottage hospital will get all the money it needs to beat the 'flu.

It may not be this year. It may not be next year. But it will be sometime.

And that is what matters, in the real world that we live in!

And can I clear up one other silly misconception that is doing the rounds in the Cool Britannia Arms?

This is NOT "The worst week since the Vicar took over the parish". Just because Mr Livingstone is being silly about the pantomime, Mr Straw has made a fool of himself at the Neighbourhood Watch meetings, Mr Cook has been giving arms rather than alms to our friends in Africa (an easy mistake!), Mr

Brown has found that there isn't as much money in the poor box as he thought, Mr Robinson is in trouble with the tax inspectors again, Mr Alan McGee, who helps with the youth club disco, has called me some childish names and the waiting list at Mr Milburn's cottage hospital has gone up again DOES NOT MEAN that this has been a bad week!

Honestly! Whatever will the tittle-tattle brigade claim next? That no one wants to go to the Millennium Tent?!

Yours ever,

Tony

The Vicar and Cherie join with parishioners in a celebration of Tony's first 1000 Days. "We're not going to sing our own praises" says Tony as he enjoys the specially-composed "Blairennium" hymn! "Alleluia!"

Confession Can Be Good For You

THE VICAR WRITES:

Confession is often under-rated in the modern world. But it can be a very liberating experience, as I discovered last week when I had a visit from a very distinguished local doctor, who is also a valued member of our congregation. For obvious reasons, I must not name him, but he is known to most of us as Dr Winston of the St Vitro's Fertility Clinic. Dr Winston had something to get off his chest. "Vicar," he said, "I have sinned against you and the church. I have been talking about you behind your back. I have accused you of hypocrisy and deceit. I have taken Cherie's name in vain. Can you ever forgive me?" I found it very touching that Dr Winston had decided to come to confession entirely of his own volition, after having had a late night visit from Mr Campbell, who had told him he knew where he lived. Of course, I forgave him without reservation, although I did warn him that if he ever stepped out of line again he might find himself in the casualty department of his own hospital!

T.B.

MILLENNIUM TENT A HUGE SUCCESS!!!

Parishioners' Postbag

Dear Vicar,

How wrong the critics are! My family and I had a marvellous day out in the Millennium Tent last Saturday. Contrary to the reports, there were no queues at all. Indeed, we had the whole place to ourselves! Our eldest boy particularly enjoyed the Asteroid Zone where he and his sister could throw ping-pong balls at each other in a recreation of the catastrophe that wiped out the dinosaurs. Well done, everyone, especially Mrs Page and her team for organising the perfect day out! And thanks to the Vicar for having such a great idea in the first place!

> *Mrs Falconer,*
> *The Old Falconry,*
> *Falcon Road.*

This is just typical of the hundreds and hundreds of letters that I have written since the tent opened. Alastair Campbell (Editor)

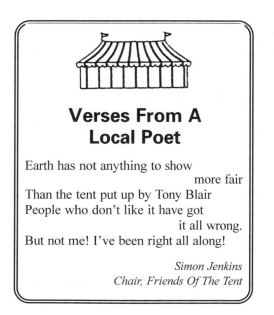

Verses From A Local Poet

Earth has not anything to show
> more fair

Than the tent put up by Tony Blair
People who don't like it have got
> it all wrong.

But not me! I've been right all along!

> *Simon Jenkins*
> *Chair, Friends Of The Tent*

ST ALBION PARISH NEWS

11th February 2000

Hullo!

I've been out and about in the parish this week, and some of you may have seen me – in my well-worn, brand new green wellington boots and Barbour jacket!

I'd heard on the grapevine – or should it be "gripevine" *(Thanks, Alastair, great joke!)* – that some members of our farming community think that they're getting a pretty raw deal these days.

So, hey! I thought, I'll go and look for myself. Talk to these guys, and show them that they're wrong!

And that's exactly what I did! And, you know, we had a very useful exchange of views!

They told me, "Vicar, we haven't got any money." And I said, "Sorry, I just don't believe you!"

And, anyway, even if they are poor – which they are not – then didn't Our Lord say "Blessed are the poor"? I mean, let's face it, everyone likes living in the countryside. It's much, much nicer than the town, particularly at weekends!

Just think of all the lovely walks you can go on, and the birds singing, and the sheep in the fields and the roaring fire blazing in the grate of a country pub!

So, honestly, what are all thse farmers complaining about, when they have a way of life that the rest of us can only envy?

Wasn't it Our Lord who said "All we like sheep"? And we do! So the farmers can be jolly grateful that they can spend all their lives surrounded with sheep (even if they can't sell them!), while the rest of us have to stay in town and earn a living!

That was my message to our farmer friends, and I have to say that they were so impressed that they listened to me in complete silence, apart from the odd "Moo from the cows" – not, as the local paper had it, "Boo from the crowd"! I'm afraid this was a typical example of the kind of sloppy journalism which is becoming far too common nowadays, particularly when they are writing about the parish and its vicar!

Apparently, there was also an unpleasant incident at the Young Farmers Club dinner where a young lady threw a chocolate eclair at Mr Brown (Nick not Gordon, unfortunately!). It was very upsetting for Nick and just went to prove that if these farmers can afford to lash out on expensive confectionery (rather than cheap

Spanish rotten tomatoes) to throw at people, then they are obviously a lot better off than they try and pretend. No more bad manners, please!

Yours,

Tony

PARISH POSTBAG

Dear Vicar,

In the light of recent events, may I suggest that the stained glass window of St Gerry the Peacemaker should be removed from the North Transept where it was installed by the Vicar last year amid much premature rejoicing, and that this empty testament to hypocrisy should be placed instead in the nearest landfill site where it should be left to

Yours faithfully,
D. TRIMBLE (MR)
Dunnegotiatin, Shankhill Road.

The Editor reserves the right to cut all letters from representatives of the forces of conservatism for reasons of space. A.C.

The real picture

OODLES OF NOODLES!

"It's the Year of the Tony" says Cherie, as she celebrates Chinese New Year at local high street restaurant the Noo Lei Bar!

✝ *To Remember In Your Prayers*

● Mrs Mowlam, who has never been quite the same since her brain operation a few years back, and who is having difficulty coming to terms with the reduced role she is having to play in the running of the parish. I know Mo used to be a very popular lady, when we all thought the Mission to St Gerry's was going to be a great success. But if things are going wrong there now, I think we know who, alas, will have to end up taking the blame! T.B.

The Millennium Tent

An Important Announcement From Mr Falconer

■ Due to the huge success of our Millennium Tent project, and the large numbers of people buying tickets, we now need some more funds to keep the project going. We shall not, of course, be drawing on parish funds for this, which would be quite wrong. We will instead be using the proceeds of our weekly parish raffle. This money was always intended to be used for charitable purposes, and what could be more charitable than giving money to the Tent? As it says in the Good Book, "Charity begins at Dome"! *(Numbers, Ch. 60 Million)* C.F.

Another Important Announcement From Mr Falconer

■ Since writing the above we have decided that the Tent is such a success it needs a new organiser. That is not to say that Mrs Page has done a bad job! It is just as it says in the Bible: "A new broom always sweeps cleaner" *(Book of Lost Job, 7.15)*

So we'd like to thank Mrs Page for all her hard work and welcome Monsieur Jean-Claude Gerbil who has kindly agreed to step in and sort out the appalling mess that Mrs Page has left.

Thanks, Jennie (for nothing!) C.F.

Clause For Thought!

THERE'S been a lot of talk around the parish about Clause 28 in the PCC Guidelines for the teachers in our primary school. Obviously, we support the family unit and it is very important that we recognise that this is a vital building block for the community. However, this is not to say that we think the old-fashioned mum/dad/kids model is in any way superior to equally valid alternative life-styles. Look, let's not be judgemental here. In my view, judgemental people are just narrow-minded bigots who should get zero-tolerance from the rest of us. That's why Mr Blunkett has got it right when he says that we should take a

 long, hard look at those guidelines; and if we think this Clause 28 has no place in today's more tolerant society, then we would be quite right to give very careful thought to reconsidering the whole issue. T.B.

HYMNS MODERN AND MODERN

(Additional Anthems and Choruses for Parish Use)

NO. 94

> *What kind of world are we living in*
> > *When old folk get mugged at night?*
> *What kind of a world are we living in*
> > *When going out gives us such a fright?*

(Chorus)

> > *We're going to get tough, tough, tough on crime*
> > *And tough on the causes of crime*
> > *(Repeat)*

> *What kind of world are we living in*
> > *When yobs get drunk in the street?*
> *What kind of world are we living in*
> > *When they push by you and tread on your feet?*

(Chorus)

> > *We're going to get tough, tough, tough on crime*
> > *And tough on the causes on crime*
> > *(Repeat)*

> *What kind of world are we living in*
> > *Where the kids take drugs for fun?*
> *What kind of world are we living in*
> > *Look: something's got to be done!*

(Chorus)

> > *We're going to get tough, tough, tough on crime*
> > *And tough on the causes on crime*
> > *(Repeat)*

(Words J. Straw)

ST ALBION PARISH NEWS

25th February 2000

Hullo!

O ye of little faith! How often I have thought of these words this week, as I considered all that has been happening in the parish recently.

Let's be absolutely frank! I have been disappointed by a lot of you, particularly those responsible for the Mission to St Gerry's.

Look. I did everything I could to make our mission a success. I even persuaded my dear friend Mr Mandelson to come out of retirement, which he was very reluctant to do.

And now Peter has had to close the whole thing down until people come to their senses.

Let me make it clear. Peter has my full support in taking this action. We all know the expression "tough love", and I think that in a very real sense Peter has been both very tough and very loving in this matter, as anyone who has seen him playing with his delightful little dog Trimble will know!

I have every confidence that, thanks to Peter's firm action in closing it down, the mission will prove to be a great success! And if it isn't, there will be no doubt who is to blame – ie, not me!

Which brings me to my second great disappointment of the week, the unfortunate removal of my friend Mr Michael as conductor of the St Albion's Welsh Male Voice Choir.

After all the trouble I had taken to get him the job in the first place, it was particularly galling that various members of the choir should have been so ungrateful as to refuse to sing under Mr Michael, and would only perform Men of Harlech under the baton of Mr Morgan, an inferior candidate for the job in every way (although he of course has my full support!).

My third disappointment of the week has been with the rest of you, for failing to appreciate what an overwhelming success our Millennium Tent has been.

Contrary to all the unpleasant rumours that have been spread around the parish, there have been no queues at the Tent, and you can get in at any time without having to wait around or be bothered by crowds.

I am particularly sorry that the children from our primary school were not allowed to join in the special "Gay Day" at the Tent, organised by Mr Smith and his partner.

I am told that the special attractions were particularly popular, including the "Cruising Zone", the "Laser Moustache Experience" and the Judy Garland record shop.

Here, surely, was an opportunity for our young people to gain first-hand understanding of alternative life-styles in a relaxed and fun setting. And what happened? 0 out of 10 to those teachers who let their prejudices get the better of them! Typical teachers!

Yours disappointedly,

Good News!!

After lengthy auditions I am pleased to announce that the part of Lord Mayor in the Christmas pantomime will be played by Mr Dobson, who for several months was in charge of looking after the sick people in the parish.

Mr Dobson was the overwhelming choice of 50.1% of the judges and I hope that now his decisive victory will put an end to the arguments and bickering which have marred this production from the very beginning.

Mr Livingstone will, I am sure, accept the unanimous decision of the casting director with good grace and any attempt on his part to start his own production will leave me with no option but to expel him from the parish. T.B.

The Second Best Man Wins

The Vicar applauds Frank as "Mayor" after last week's decisive vote

Parish Appointments

■ After the tremendous success Mr Falconer has made of the Tent, I have decided to enlarge his responsibilities by asking him to take over some of the duties at present performed by Mr Prescott. It is not that Mr Prescott has been doing his job badly. It is just that he has not been doing it very well. I am glad to say that Mr Falconer has become a great asset to the parish, which I always knew he would be since he is my oldest friend.

LETTERS TO THE EDITOR

Dear Sir,

In answer to your query last month (Parish Poser, Jan. 31) as to who should be on the empty plinth in the square, may I suggest that there is only one possible candidate, the Vicar!

Yours sincerely
John Birt,
Waheed Ali,
David Puttnam,
Melvyn Bragg,
Matthew Evans,
Andrew Motion

Sunrise Home For Friends Of Tony (formerly Sunset Home For Retired Gentlefolk)

The Editor writes: This is only one of hundreds of letters we have received making the same point! A.C.

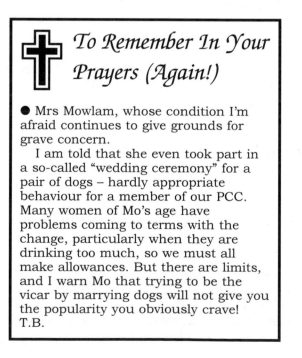

✝ To Remember In Your Prayers (Again!)

● Mrs Mowlam, whose condition I'm afraid continues to give grounds for grave concern.

I am told that she even took part in a so-called "wedding ceremony" for a pair of dogs – hardly appropriate behaviour for a member of our PCC. Many women of Mo's age have problems coming to terms with the change, particularly when they are drinking too much, so we must all make allowances. But there are limits, and I warn Mo that trying to be the vicar by marrying dogs will not give you the popularity you obviously crave!
T.B.

ST ALBION PARISH NEWS

10th March 2000

Hullo!

And, of course, there's been only one topic of conversation in the parish this week – and that's the great party we had in the church hall to celebrate the first 100 years of St Albion's!

What an unforgettable evening it was – and special thanks to all the ladies of the parish, led by Cherie, who worked so hard behind the scenes to make all the refreshments!

Mr Sainsbury's "Holy Guacamole" GM Dip went down particularly well – as did his tomatofish soup!

And what a pleasure it was to welcome back so many old faces from the parish's long history, some of whom we hadn't seen for many a long day!

I was very sad not to have had more time to talk to Canon Foot, the Very Rev. Callaghan and Mr Kinnock, who used to be our lay preacher.

It was touching that they all wanted to come up to give me their ideas. And, no doubt, in the friendliest possible way, they would have wanted to suggest that things were better in their day!

That's old people for you! They always look back on the past with rose-tinted spectacles. But when you look at it, you usually find the reality was very different.

Take Canon Foot, for example. He's a sweet old soul, with his white hair, his walking stick and his little dog.

But, frankly, if he'd been allowed to run the parish, the pews would soon have been empty and the whole place would have been shut down!

As for Rev. Callaghan, well, no offence to Jim, but he was the worst vicar this parish has ever had! And that's being kind! If it wasn't for the fact that his daughter Margaret is now one of the most respected members of the parish team, and really getting things moving in the Sunrise Home For Friends Of The Vicar (formerly the Sunset Home For Distressed Gentlefolk), I might have a lot more to say on this topic!

Look. It's all very well getting nostalgic about the way things used to be done in the old days. But the fact is no one's really interested in all that stuff any more.

At the party, it was noticeable that most people didn't know the words of those dreary old Victorian hymns some people wanted to sing, such as "There Is A Red Flag Far Away". But I think myself that's a good sign, because it means we're looking forward to the future! And the future is now!

In fact, it's been the future for the last three years! Ever since I took over. It's about time some of these old people realised it, and stayed away!

Incidentally, I would like to make it clear that I never recommended parishioners to eat Mr Sainsbury's GM guacamole or tomatofish soup!

I always made it clear that while, on the one hand, GM foods could clearly be enormously beneficial to mankind and very tasty, on the other hand, it is quite possible that they could be highly toxic and destructive to the environment.

That has been my position all along, and you could not want a clearer statement than that! So much for the people who say I can't make my mind up!

And before I finish, I would just like to commend the wonderful poem elsewhere in this newsletter penned by my very good friend, Melvyn!

Yours,

Tony

100th Birthday Party

Three of our pensioners take part in a special version of the popular TV game Blind Date. In our version "Blind Dotage" parishioners had to choose which of the three was best suited to run the parish. The answer was Number Four, of course: The Vicar! T.B.

Verses By A Local Poet

In Defence Of Tony

All the knockers are out for Tony,
They call him a traitor and a phoney.
They even say that I'm a "crony",
But I say that is just "baloney"!

Tony Blair is a perfect wonder,
He's not committed a single blunder!
Tony is handsome, nice and clever,
And, what's more, he's the best vicar ever!

M. Barg, South Bankside.

✝ To Remember In Your Prayers

● Rosalind Mark, who has let everyone down very badly after she worked as a nanny at the vicarage and then sold her story to the St Albion Messenger. Pray that she may be taken to court and punished severely with the full rigour of the law and be forced to repay any moneys paid to her and then made to serve a custodial sentence of three terms of life to run concurrently. May God forgive her because Cherie and I will find it very difficult to do so. T.B.

☠ NOTICE ☠

A SERVICE OF EXCOMMUNICATION WILL BE HELD NEXT SUNDAY

Mr Ken Livingstone will be cast into utter darkness. Kids, please bring a candle! T.B.

MILLENNIUM TENT LATEST

Half-term was a tremendous success for the tent. Hundreds of children had to be turned away. Well done everyone concerned (especially our new French friend M. Gerbil who has come over to help out with the car parking arrangements). T.B.

Thought For The Week

*A*MID all the silly tittle-tattle about the choice of our friend Mr Dobson to play the part of the Lord Mayor of London in this year's St Albion's pantomime being rigged and "a fix", let me remind parishioners what it says in the Good Book, "The first shall be last, and the last first". So, the fact is that since Mr Livingstone came first in the popularity stakes, and Mr Dobson was last, the Bible tells us that Mr Dobson should be the winner. And I hope no one is going to argue with Holy Scripture! T.B.

ST ALBION PARISH NEWS

24th March 2000

Hullo,

Well, Lent is with us once again – and I'm sure we all enjoyed our new GM-free pancakes, a huge improvement on last year's genetically modified pancakes supplied by Mr Sainsbury, which some of us felt tasted rather too strongly of mackerel!

I wonder what all of you have given up for Lent this year? If you have not yet decided, may I offer a few suggestions?

One idea which I hope will gain favour is that people should give up complaining about those in positions of authority in our parish, who are only trying to do the job as well as I can, in what are, frankly, very difficult circumstances.

And let's not just give it up for the prescribed 40 days. Let's give it up all through the year, and then we could really start to get things moving here at St. Albion's.

I don't want to name names, but I am sure Mr Kilfoyle will know who I have in mind – not to mention Mr Livingstone, who is no longer a member of the parish after his disgraceful behaviour in putting himself forward for the role of Lord Mayor in the pantomime, even after I had made it quite clear that I did not want him.

And now I gather that Mr Livingstone has been complaining that I am trying to smear him, by dragging up details of his private life.

This is frankly ridiculous. It is not my job as a vicar to tell everyone that Mr Livingstone has not been entirely open about how he earns his living and has also been sleeping around with various younger female members of the congregation! Even if these things were true, which they are, it is no concern of mine that he has been falsifying his tax returns and jumping into bed with all the ladies on the flower roster!

And another thing which some members of the congregation should give up are their beards.

We have long since moved on from the old-fashioned idea of God as an old man with a white beard. We now see him as a young man without a beard.

Which is why Mr Dobson will need to shave his beard off very soon, if he is to make any impression in the forthcoming pantomime.

Remember, as it says in the Bible, "I Esau am a smooth man, but my brother Dobbo is an hairy man." And guess which of them became ruler? Look it up in the *Book of Follicles*, 7.3

And what am I giving up, you may be wondering. The answer is, this letter! (Who says I haven't got a sense of humour!)

Yours

Tony

ANNOUNCEMENTS

Mr Straw from the Neighbourhood Watch reports that there have been a number of Romanian women begging in and around the churchyard. Whilst Mr Straw appreciates that some old-fashioned parishioners might feel sorry for these women he would remind them of the words of the text "Charity Begins At Calais" (*Book of Enoch, 14.2*). Mr Straw feels rightly that the most charitable response is to deport anyone dressed in a headscarf immediately! Thanks to Mrs Widdecombe (not normally one of Mr Straw's fans!) for her suggestion on the church noticeboard that "hanging is too good for them".

Well done, Mr Brown, for presenting his annual accounts of the parish finances to the open meeting! He told everyone that they were actually giving less money to the church even if when they counted it up it seemed to be more! They may be poorer, he said, but they are a lot better off! So, good for Mr Brown, who has shown again how well he can implement the excellent ideas of his superior(s). T.B.

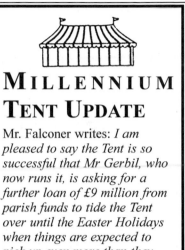

MILLENNIUM TENT UPDATE

Mr. Falconer writes: *I am pleased to say the Tent is so successful that Mr Gerbil, who now runs it, is asking for a further loan of £9 million from parish funds to tide the Tent over until the Easter Holidays when things are expected to pick up even more than they have done already. The other good news is the Tent is so successful that we have decided to keep it open all night in the hope that a few drunks will stumble in by mistake and we can charge them for going to the toilet* (Are you sure you want this last bit in? A.C.) *Also, it is great news that Bob Ayling, who has been largely responsible for the success of the Tent, has taken voluntary dismissal from the travel agent where he worked in the High Street. This means that Bob will now have even more time to devote to the Tent, which must be good news!*

PARABLES FOR MODERN MAN (AND WOMAN!)

As retold by the Vicar

Now there were two groups of virgins living in that time. The one had consisted of wise virgins, who had taken unto themselves the internet. And they did keep awake day and night accessing information on all manner of subjects. But the other virgins were foolish and had no web. And their lives were empty and they had no e-mail. And when the great day came and the Bridegroom arrived, the wise virgins were prepared for his coming. For they had downloaded his arrival time from www.lastminutebridegroom.com. But the foolish virgins who had been sitting around reading books and doing the housework were not ready, and missed out on a very important opportunity. T.B.

✝ *To Remember In Your Prayers*

● My sister-in-law Lauren, who I am sorry to say is having severe mental problems, during the course of which she said some very nasty things about her sister, including a description of Cherie as a "trophy wife", whatever that may be. Help her to realise that a period of silence and a large dose of God's gift of Valium would do her no end of good in her deranged state. T.B.

Mr Blunkett telling the vicar about the three Rs – "Rong, Rong and Rong"! Good for David for admitting his errors about "selection" and three cheers for St Albion's Grammar – always the Vicar's favourite school*.
*This was true at the time of printing. A. Campbell (Editor)

ST ALBION PARISH NEWS

7th April 2000

Hullo!

Well, there's certainly only one thing I can write about this week, judging from my postbag!

I cannot remember any ethical issue causing such heated debate in the parish as the one which is now occupying all our thoughts, as we look forward to a certain happy event in May! Should your vicar take time off to be with Cherie and their new baby Tony (or Tonella)!?

On the one hand, there are those of you who say that a vicar's first duty is to his flock, and that he should carry on with all his duties running the parish. Particularly when none of his colleagues is up to the task of standing in for him (no offence John, Gordon, David, Jack, Stephen, Mo, etc).

On the other hand, there are those of you (including Cherie) who say "Look, this is the 21st century. Isn't it the first duty of any man to be at the side of his wife or partner, at such an important moment – the beginning of a new life!"

Isn't this what they call a Catch 28 situation? Heads I lose, tails you win!

Whatever I do, I am going to be criticised. On the one hand, our friend in Tesco will be standing by the nappy counter, telling me that I should be getting back to the work I am paid to do.

On the other hand, some aggressive working women with high-flying careers in such fields as the Law may well be shouting at me in the middle of the night to go and make a cup of tea for the nanny!

And who is to say which of these options is the best one?

But I think there is a third way, as there so often is in life! And the third way in this case is simple. I won't make a decision either way until the last minute, when I see what most people in the parish think.

To make your views known to me, Mr Campbell has printed a special slip after this letter for you all to fill in. Please send it in to the vicarage as soon as possible, and remember it is a SECRET ballot (ie, Cherie will not see it).

Yours in hope!

Tony

SHOULD TONY TAKE PATERNITY LEAVE?

I THINK

☐ A. The Vicar should concentrate on his important duties running the parish as only he knows how.

☐ B. The Vicar should waste his time hanging around at home, getting in everyone's way, when he should be back in his office running the parish.

Verses By A Local Poet

Reasons To Be Cheerful

(with apologies to the late Ian Dury)

1. Tony
2. Tony
3. Tony
4. The Vicar
5. Rev. A. Blair
6. Cherie's Husband
7. Father of Baby Tony (or Tonella)

A. Motion, St Albion's Parish Poet

THE TENT IN LENT

Thanks to our good friend Mr Gerbil for coming up with a brilliant suggestion as to how we can all celebrate Easter. Go to the Tent!

He is confidently expecting record crowds over the holiday, which is why he is making a special Family Ticket Offer – Buy One, Get Twenty Free!

Lenten Talk

What it Means to be a St Albion-ite

In this, the third of his Lenten addresses, the Vicar will consider those qualities which make the people of this parish of ours so uniquely St Albionish:

- tolerance
- hard work
- respect for leaders
- obedience to authority
- disinclination to argue with those in charge.

Attendance at this talk in the Church Hall is of course voluntary, but Mr Campbell will be taking names at the door.
You have been warned! A.C.

The St Albion's Home for Distressed Gentlefolk

The Matron, Mrs Jay, writes:

I am sick of listening to people complaining about our admissions policy. It is not true that to gain entry to the Home you have to be either very rich or a friend of the Vicar's. We have made it quite clear that you have to be both. I hope that clears the matter up once and for all.

Mrs Jay (née Callaghan), Matron, The People's Home, St Albion's.

 Parish Postbag

Dear Vicar,

In all my long years as a loyal supporter of St Albion's I never imagined a day when I would find myself accusing the Vicar of destroying the integrity of our faith. Yet, only yesterday he gave a hundred places in the Old Folks Home to his personal
Yours faithfully,
Tony Benn,
Tetley House, PG T1PS.
The Editor reserves the right to cut letters in the interests of the Vicar.

✝ To Remember In Your Prayers

- Poor Sarah Macaulay, whom I understand has been very badly let down by her boyfriend.

  After leading her on for many years with promises of marriage, and even being photographed together with children for the benefit of the local paper, she has now been "dumped down", as I believe the expression is. Let us pray that Sarah does not fall for the temptation of forgiveness, but makes it known in the strongest possible way how she feels about mean, dour, workaholic Scotsmen who cannot commit themselves to anything! T.B.

ST ALBION PARISH NEWS

21st April 2000

Hullo!

Once again there's only one topic that anyone is talking about, as we approach the festival of Easter!

And that's the new life that's going to come into being in the vicarage in just a few weeks' time!

And how perfect it is that it should be just at this time of the year, when we are all thinking about eggs, and bunnies and fluffy chicks, that Cherie should have decided that we should have our own equivalent of all those little lambs frolicking round the meadows and speaking to us the message of what the Bible calls "New life, new hope, new Labour" *(Letter To The Mandelsonians, 7.3).*

You may remember last week I was talking about the all-important moral choice that all us husbands, or rather partners (of either sex of course!), have to face on this sort of occasion.

Should I take time off, or should I just carry on working?

You won't be surprised that, confronted with these two alternatives, I have come up with a "third way" which provides a way out of the problem.

I will not be at my desk. But nor will I be making tea for the nanny!

I will be "in holiday mode," which means that I will be working some of the time, and will be making myself available to help the nanny if she needs me!

This is a thoroughly modern compromise, which I hope will satisfy everyone, whatever their view – although I suspect our friend from the Tesco checkout queue will still find something to gripe about!

Talking of which, I have been saddened by the rather negative reaction of many parishioners, who have attended rehearsals of our St Albion's pantomime, towards Mr Dobson's performance in the role of Lord Mayor of London.

I personally think Frank is brilliant in the part, and everyone who says he is absolutely useless and can't even remember his lines will, I am sure, be proved wrong on the night.

He will be fantastic. And anyone who says "Oh no, he won't" has not got into the spirit of things at all!

A very happy Christmas to you all! Tony

A Message For Good Friday

From Mr Mandelson, head of the Mission to St Gerry's:

This is the time of year of course when we remember the Good Friday agreement, which the vicar did so much to bring about. That was the day when we all solemnly buried our differences. And some people are now saying that after only three days they came back to life. But this is not true. The whole point of Good Friday is that once things are buried they stay buried! P.M.

Confession

The Vicar will be taking confessions over the Easter period if anyone wishes to seek absolution (Mr Brown, Mr Byers and Mrs Short may be interested!). The Vicar does, however, wish to make it clear that he has made his own confession to the local newspaper – and in it he has freely admitted his mistake in not initially choosing Mr Rhodri Morgan to lead the Welsh Male (and Female!) Voice Choir.

"I am not perfect," Tony told the St Albion Messenger, "and it is not my fault that Mr Michael was useless and let me down badly. I am wrong to blame myself for this and confess that sometimes I just try too hard to serve the parish."

Alastair Campbell

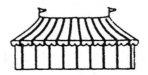

Millennium Tent Update

A message from M. Gerbil, our Tent Supremo, who will be writing the updates in the newsletter in future rather than Mr Falconer

Allo, tout le monde! Le tent est un succes enorme, faites-vous no mistake! Which is pourquoi, pour le vacance d'Easter, nous offerons un Tres Special Deal pour toute la famille. Admissions absolument LIBRE pendant les heures 8am-12pm.

Un jour to remember pour tout le lifetime!
Jean-Claude Gerbil

P.S. Mes apologies profondes a tous les crediteurs de la Tente! Patience, gentilhommes! Les cheques sont dans la poste, je vous assure! *J-C.G.*

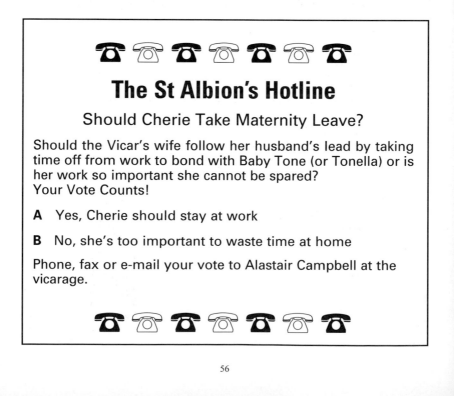

The St Albion's Hotline

Should Cherie Take Maternity Leave?

Should the Vicar's wife follow her husband's lead by taking time off from work to bond with Baby Tone (or Tonella) or is her work so important she cannot be spared?
Your Vote Counts!

A Yes, Cherie should stay at work

B No, she's too important to waste time at home

Phone, fax or e-mail your vote to Alastair Campbell at the vicarage.

NEW RESPONSES FOR EVENSONG

Just a reminder that from now on we'll be using a slightly revised set of responses in the normal service.

Here they are – so please do commit them to memory so everyone knows what's going on. T.B.

CONGREGATION:
All good things that are on earth

VICAR:
I want to be personally associated with them

CONGREGATION:
All the good things that are in the heavens

VICAR:
I want to be personally associated with them

CONGREGATION:
All good things that are in the sea

VICAR:
I want to be personally associated with them

CONGREGATION:
All eye-catching initiatives, all that is modern and new and popular and on the web

VICAR:
I want to be personally associated with them

ALL:
Amen

ST ALBION PARISH NEWS

5th May 2000

Hullo!

And what a sad week it has been for all of us!

As those of you who were there will know all too well, the opening night of the pantomime was a disaster.

When Mr. Dobson came on as Mayor of London, he was literally booed off stage.

And, you know, in my heart of hearts, I couldn't really blame the audience.

I don't in any way want to be judgmental but Frank was completely useless.

He got his lines all wrong. He could not be heard at the back of the hall.

His trousers fell down in the important scene when the bells rang out to announce who would be Lord Mayor.

Even the stuffed cat was more entertaining than Frank. I don't want to go on about how bad he was, and I write this more in sorrow than in anger!

But I am very angry indeed about how badly Frank has let me down.

If he didn't want the job he should have said so when I told him he had to do it!

As it was, he didn't even try! And when the scenery fell down when he walked into it, I have to confess that I booed as loudly as everyone else!

The consequence was inevitable. When my old friend Mr. Livingstone jumped up onto the stage to take over the part, the audience quite rightly laughed and cheered.

And don't get me wrong. I cheered with the rest of them!

When Ken got up and made his little joke about this being 'one in the eye for the vicar', I was the first to join in the laughter!

Ken and I may have had our differences in the past, particularly when I excommunicated him from St. Albion's, but deep down we share the same beliefs! Ours is a broad church, and we can do business together.

My door is always open, Ken, and there is a glass of sherry waiting on the sideboard!

As the children of the St. Albion's Primary School sang in the panto:

The bells of Big Ben
Say "Welcome Red Ken"
The Bells of old Bow
Say "Get lost Dobbo"

So 'Turn again Livingstone', and welcome back to the fold!
Your friend

Tony

"Mr Livingstone, I presume!"
– Panto Fun last Thursday

✉ Parish Postbag

From the Rev. R. Mugabe in our sister church of
Our Lady of the Machetes, Harare

Dear Sir,
Your vicar and his cronies are just a load of shirtlifters and
bottom bandits! Let me tell you, I have nothing but contempt for you,
Mr. Gayboy Blair, and your boyfriend Gordon.
Yours sincerely
Bob Mugabe

This letter has been cut for reasons of space. A.C.

Notice From The Vicar

Like everyone else I was disgusted by the mindless youths who ripped up the vicarage lawn over the May Day holiday. I want everyone to know that I am totally opposed to this sort of behaviour.

I can think of no words to describe the yobs except yobs, and possibly Conservatives. *(Are you sure? A.C.)* And as for defacing the statue of the Very Reverend Churchill – have they no respect for the past? No feeling for the history of this great parish of ours? No time for traditional values? No, they are yobs. That is the only word for them. As it says in the Good Book, "It's not funny and it's not clever" *(The Acts of Violence, Ch. 3, vs. 7-8)*

A Message From Mr. Mandelson

I would like to take this opportunity to scotch all the silly rumours (which have been put about by me) that I am dissatisfied with my boring and depressing job at the St. Gerry's Mission, and would like to return to the vicar's side, to plan the next exciting phase in the great St. Albion's project.

I have certainly achieved a great deal here in Ireland, particularly when I had to close down the mission and told everyone to go home. And it may be that the vicar decides that there is nothing more for me to do, and that any remaining loose ends can be tied up by a lesser member of the team. But that is entirely a matter for the vicar to decide. Over to you Tony!

P.M.

P.S. If anyone has any agreeable flats for sale in the centre of town, I have a friend who might soon be relocating and looking for somewhere to live as near to the vicarage as possible.

Millennium Tent Update

A Message From Monsieur Gerbil

JE suis tres sorry to say que l'Easter Weekend n'etait pas le grand succes que nous hoped for. Helas, je blame votre English weather (ou les showers d'April, n'est-ce pas?). Personne wants to go inside quand il est raining, non? Ca c'est pourquoi seulement trois of ze 8000 tickets nous hoped vendre pendant le weekend d'Easter etaient actuellement purchased. Quel dommage! Mais il faut regarder sur le bright side! Bientot il sera le summertime, et le soleil will brille, et tout le monde sera boarding L'Eurostar pour un happy vacance dans la belle France. Ah! La gaie Paree! La tour Eiffel! Ooh, la, la – les demoiselles topless de St Tropez! Ou peut-etre une gite agreable en Provence, comme votre Peter Mayle! Oh, mon dieu, je wish j'etais back chez moi instead of sitting in cette horrible tente avec le vicaire et le lack de punters et

This update from M. Gerbil has had to be cut short for reasons of space. A.C.

ST ALBION PARISH NEWS

19th May 2000

Hi!

And a bit of a depressing week it's been, to be frank (and when I say "frank", you know who I mean!).

Do you know how many people turned out for our May Day Flower Festival and Songs of Praise?

I will tell you. Just four! And that represents only 0.005 percent of the parish register.

And I think I know the reason why some people in the parish have not been quite as supportive lately as they should have been!

It's all to do with cynicism, which comes from two Greek words "sin" and "schism".

And that's what it means. The sin of setting yourself up as separate from the right and true way of doing things!

A cynic is someone who may be jolly clever, but who, deep down, doesn't believe in anything.

We all know people like that, don't we? People who go on about how much better things were in the old days. Or people who pretend that poor people need help and that rich people should have all their money taken away from them.

Well, that is just the sort of thinking that I've been trying to change in my three years here at St Albion's.

As it says in the New Labour Bible, "For he has kept the mighty in their seats, and the poor he hath sent empty away" *(Gospel according to St Luke Johnson).*

That's the Third Way I've been trying to put across. That's what I believe in.

But what do the cynics believe in? Nothing! It's just knock, knock, knock, all the time!

Frankly (no, not him!) I'd rather have young William Hague, who at least believes all that nonsense he talks in our Sixth Form Debating Society, even if everything he says is completely wrong!*

So, let's make this our message for the rest of this Millennium Year.

It's not just the forces of conservatism we have to fight, but the equally powerful and destructive forces of cynicism.

Our job is to go out into the parish and spread the good news!

As we sing in the moving chorus I wrote for last week's third anniversary evensong:

"We've done a lot
    But there's much left to do
So let's not blame Tony
    If we're feeling kinda blue."

Yours,

Tony

*Young William did not win the debate last week, by the way, even though it might have helped if some of the PCC had briefed me a little better beforehand on some of the trickier points he raised!

Millennium Tent Update

From Jean-Claude Gerbil

Mes amis,

Je suis un peu desperate. Personne, mais PERSONNE, ne vient to the Tent over les trois recent Banque Holidays. Pourquoi? je demande. Après tout, c'était completely free pour les enfants, et aussi pour leurs parents. Peut-être c'est le "wrong kind of tent", comme vous dites en Angleterre, n'est-ce pas? Now, j'ai une idée très brilliante pour attracter les missing millions.

Si vous visitez le tent nous payer vous 100 euros per personne (6p). Puis-je dire fairer que ça, squire?

Rollez-up punteurs pour l'experience d'un lifetime. J-C.G.

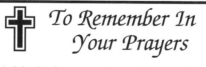

✝ *To Remember In Your Prayers*

● Mr Dobson, whom I hope is not feeling too low after letting everyone down so badly in the pantomime. May he come to realise that his prospects of future service in the parish are now nil after such a lamentable performance! Help him to go off into the wilderness with grace and dignity, and never to be heard of again! T.B.

Notices

The vicar is shortly to take his paternity leave, which is not paternity leave at all, but a relaxed holiday period in which he will still be available to run the country as well as change the odd nanny *(Is this right? A.C.)*, and he has been asked by many parishioners "Who is in charge, Tony?" The answer is a simple one. Mr Prescott from the Working Men's Club will be in charge of day-to-day matters unless anything important occurs in the vicar's semi-absence. In that case, Mr Prescott will refer the matter upwards, ie to Mr Campbell. I hope that is clear. T.B.

Hats off to Cherie as she wins the Boy George lookalike competition at the May Day Flower Festival!

Talking Point

● You know, computers are the future! No doubt about it! I want to see a parish in which every home is on the net, and every child in our local schools has a PC on his or her desk, from which they can download all the riches of the world's knowledge. It is a truly exciting voyage of discovery for every young mind!

Yet there are dangers. I know, from watching my own kids, as they sit at home staring vacantly at the screen for hours on end, or surfing mindlessly through some "chat room", how destructive these computers can be of family life and the normal give-and-take of human relationships.

That is why I am coming round to the view that all computers should be banned, both in schools and homes, so that we can all rediscover the old-fashioned pleasure of eating family meals round the TV!

You know, I'm getting quite cynical about the whole internet thing! T.B.

A Special Message From The Vicar

A BIG "HI" from your weary, but ever so happy vicar!

And a "hi" from little Leo too, who's looking forward to meeting you all!

And a big, big "thank you" from the amazing Cherie, for all the thousands of lovely cards and flowers that you've sent me since our Great News!

What can I say? Leo is a great little kid! Just gorgeous! And, as I told you before, I'll be taking a few days off to look after him and catch up on my sleep!

So, it's over now to John, our Parish No. 2, whom I've asked to look after the shop (or should I say "ship", in John's case?) in my absence.

Missing you already!

Tony

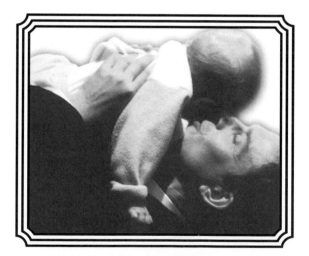

Remember the words of the Prophet "The Lion (Leo!) shall lie down with the Vicar" *(Book of Posea, 11.3)*

FROM THE WORKING MEN'S CLUB

May I be the first to congratulate Tony and Cherie on their happy event?

But let's not get things out of proportion, shall we?

It's only a baby after all. And a lot of us have had a few of those in our time without making a great song and dance about it, and calling in the local paper!

Tony decided to be in at the birth, which of course is entirely his decision.

But some of the older parishioners might wonder – and who can blame them – whether it wouldn't have been a damn sight more useful if Tony had stayed back at the vicarage to get on with the work he's paid to do, rather than poncing about in a denim shirt looking like a cross between a male model and a tea-boy, as some unkind person might well have said!

I don't want to disparagise Tony's efforts to be modern and with it.

But if I'd lain down full length on the carpet posing with any of my kids, I think Pauline might have said "Get up, you daft booger" *(pardon my French!)*, "or everyone'll think you're a poof" *(pardon my Italian!)*.

Each to his own, is what it says in the Good Book, and it would be a dull world indeed if we were all as sensible as me!

So, let's not begrudgerate the Vicar his little moment of glory, and I'm sure we're all very sympathetic with Cherie having to put up with all this crying and bleating (and that's just Tony – no offence, Tone, just having a bit of fun!).

But at least one good thing has come out of all this ridiculous nuss and fonsense, and that's that I've been given a chance to take over again, as I'm always happy to do, and sort out some of the messes that certain people have left behind them!

Cheers!

JoHN

John Prescott

Poem on the Birth of Leo Blair

Welcome, baby, to our world,
Let all the flags be now unfurled,
And as you gasp the sweet May air
We all salute you Leo Blair.

I'd like to have penned a second verse,
And one that wouldn't have been much worse,
But as you know, I'm fantastically busy,
Doing important jobs that would make anyone
else feel dizzy.

Lord Melvyn of Barg,
Southbank House

PS. I enclose a self-billing
invoice for the sum of £10,000.

Millennium Tent

A Special Message From Our Millennium Tent Organiser, Monsieur Jean-Claude Gerbil

Mes Amis de St Albion!

Un grand merci à Monsieur Falconer (et naturellement aussi le Vicar!) pour le cheque enorme (£28.75p!) pour la continuation de la Tente Millenaire pour un autre week!

Quand le cheque arrived, comme je said à Madame Gerbil, "Vraiement, this is one amazing day!" Et surement, c'est une vote de confidence dans mes abilités to make la Tente an even plus grand success.

Indeed, je peux annoncer nous avons des new targets. From aujourd'hui nous avons decidés que three or four personnes visitant la tente chaque jour will be counted as "meeting le target". Et voilà, nous sommes meeting our nouveau target already!

J-C. Gerbil

PS. Au revoir à M. Ayling, et un big thank you pour all vous avez fait to make la Tente le grand success! Et bienvenu M. Quarmby. Comme ils disent dans votre country, "Crazy name, crazy guy," n'est-ce pas?

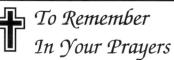

✝ To Remember In Your Prayers

● Gordon Brown who has made a bit of a fool of himself by talking nonsense about St Albion's Comprehensive School. Let us pray that in future he does a bit of homework before opening his mouth! Perhaps he is in need of a long holiday – though without any family commitments (not even a girlfriend!) it is probably a bit hard to justify!

T.B.

ALMS-GIVING

Mr Cook Writes:

We are holding a jumble sale in the Parish Hall on Bank Holiday Monday to raise funds to provide the children of Sierra Leone with much needed guns:

£5 will buy a box of ammunition

£10 will buy a 2nd-hand armalite rifle

£50 will buy a machine gun.

All jumble welcome (except copies of my ex-wife Margaret's book which no one wants to buy because it is not of interest at all).

R. Cook

AN ANGRY MESSAGE FROM THE EDITOR MR ALASTAIR CAMPBELL

I am disgusted, as I am sure all right-thinking decent parishioners are, by the discourteous and unforgiveable treatment meted out to the Vicar by the so-called ladies of St Albion's WI last week.

The Vicar, having just returned from his paternity leave, had generously asked if he could address the meeting, only to be greeted with cat-calls, slow hand-claps and jeering. This behaviour was a disgrace. There is no excuse for such rudeness, above all to the Vicar, who has done so much for all these ladies in the church hall.

Obviously, the Vicar is sorry he could not get his message across about the importance of Damson Jam and Lemon Drizzle Cake in today's parish. In fact, he had spent weeks if not minutes preparing his remarks.

And he is sorry that the audience decided not to listen to his uncontentious recipe for Meat Loaf Salad.

In a spirit of Christian forgiveness, the Vicar has decided to close down the Women's Institute forthwith and to ban the following ladies from the Flower Rota for life: Mrs E. Titmarsh, Mrs J. Bulstrode, Mrs C. Bradford-Ffrench, Lady Custard (Ms), Mrs S. Dalrymple, Fran Wittgenstein-Himmler, Mrs Chapatti, the late Dame Witherington-Bakewell, and many others too numerous to mention here. There will be a full list of names and addresses posted at the back of the church. Please check to see if you are one of the rude ladies who ruined the Vicar's first day back.

Here is the speech (written by the Vicar himself) that you would have heard if it had not been for the disruptive minority of women who formed the majority of the audience.

Hello Ladies,

Nice to see you all in your lovely summer dresses and hats. Let's hope you keep them on. *(Pause for laughter.)* But seriously I know how busy you good ladies are with your jam-making and collecting clothes for the jumble sale, so it's very good of you to allow me to tell you how well everything is going in the parish as a result of my hard work. *(Pause for applause.)*

And Leo says hello. *(Pause for cries of "Aaah!".)*

But I came here with a message and what I want you all to take forward in your lives is simply this: let's not abandon all those traditional values which made St Albion's what it is today. *(Look serious.)*

It's all very easy to mock those values, in the scramble to be new and modern. But, let's face it, you don't want to throw out the baby with the bathwater (a lesson I've been trying to teach the nanny over the past fortnight!). *(Pause for more laughter.)*

I think of all those good people sitting in the middle of the church – solid, dependable, respectable people, with their families, their sense of decency and their respect for law and order.

People like our good friend Mr Dacre, who coincidentally edits one of our most popular local papers, the St Albion's Mail. And people like you!!

Heaven forbid that we should offend good, honest folk, who could easily drift away from the church if they sense that, say, the sillier views about "class" expressed by Mr Brown or Mr Prescott carried any weight with the Vicar. But they don't! *(Bang fist on lectern.)*

So let's start a real crusade for the commonsense values of yesteryear! *(Acknowledge cheers.)*

Let us root out the forces of modernism wherever we find them!

As it says in the Book of Oddbin, "You should not pour new wine into old bottles. It's old wine you want, every time." And old ladies too!

God bless you and Good Afternoon!

(Standing Ovation.)

Recipe Of The Week

Here's a recipe from a really sensible working woman who hasn't got time to cook (or to sit around being rude to important speakers)

CHERIE'S CHERRY PIE

- ☛ Put Sainsbury's GM-Free Cherry Pie in microwave.
- ☛ Set dial for 3 minutes at power ten.
- ☛ Ping! Pie's nice and ever so hot! (Serves 2)

DO YOU KNOW ANY OF THESE WOMEN? IF SO, THE NEIGHBOURHOOD WATCH WOULD LIKE TO HEAR FROM YOU. ANSWERS WILL BE TREATED IN STRICT CONFIDENCE. RING ST ALBION'S 73742723.

✝ *To Remember In Your Prayers*

Mrs Jay, the matron of the St Albion's Old People's Home, who has unfortunately been caught out telling lies about where she went to school. Help her to understand that it is not clever or helpful to pretend that you have been to the local Grammar School, when in fact you went to the St Albion's High School For Young Ladies (fees £5000 a term), and that this kind of thing reflects very badly on the person who was brave enough to give her the job when there were not a few people who said that, frankly, she wasn't up to it! T.B.

Millennium Tent Update

from Jean-Claude Gerbil

Bonjour, mes amis! Et cette semaine, good news! Comme vous will remember, last week nous avons revisés le target pour le numéro de visiteurs à la Grande Tente. Voici un petit chart pour illustrer notre succès énorme!

Target Visiteurs	Actuel Visiteurs
0	0

Eh voila! Nous avons achieved le target! Pas mal, n'est-ce pas? Merci pour votre support. Et souvenez, la tente est ouverte tous les jours (et les nuits), admission absolument libre pour tous les personnes aged entre 0 et 100.

J-C. Gerbil
Grand Supremo de la Tente

Parish Postbag

Dear Sir,
Hats off to Gordon Brown for blowing the gaffe on all t'poncy boogers with their fancy ways and hoity-toity Oxbridge degrees pontificating in lahdidah voices about

Yours sincerely,
J. Prescott,
Working Men's
Stately Home,
Dorneywood,
Bucks.

PS. I have told the butler to deliver this by hand, and sent him round in the spare Jag.

Apologies

The Vicar has apologised to the following people this week on your behalf for their terrible treatment at the hands of society:

The Guildford Four
The Jackson Five
The Birmingham Six
Blake's 7

ANNOUNCEMENTS

● The hymn "Jerusalem" will be removed from the Hymn Book – Hymns Modern and New (1999).

● The visiting lay preacher Mr Gyles Brandreth will not be welcome at any parish event until further notice.

● The Vicar will be back to write his normal letter next week – *if* everyone behaves. A.C.

HYMNS MODERN AND MODERN

(Additional Anthems and Choruses for Parish Use)

No. 95
TO BE SUNG AT THE WORKING MEN'S CLUB ONLY

There is a green hill far away
Without a city wall
Where we can site 2000 homes
With garages for all.
We may not know, we cannot tell
How much it all will cost,
But of one thing we can be sure
The countryside will be lost.

(Words J. Prescott)

No. 96
TRADITIONAL CAROL FOR CHILDREN

Little foxy, little foxy,
With your bushy tail,
Keep on going, keep on going
Safely down the trail.

We won't hunt you
We won't chase you,
You can live in peace.
We won't hunt you,
We won't chase you,
You can kill those geese.

(Words K. Livingstone)

Parish Scrapbook

A look at events in St Albion's over the last year
Compiled by Alastair Campbell

The Vicar stresses the importance of new technology "I am the information highway, the truth and the life" *(St Paul's e-mail to the Corinthians)*

The Vicar drops in on one of the House Focus Groups (Thanks, Mrs Harris!) with his message for Lent: "Trust me or you'll end up in the wilderness for 40 years" *(Book of Worzel, 17.5)*

The Vicar and French padré Father Jospin emerge from church together. As you can see there's no "beef" between them. You could almost call it a "joint" service

Things are looking up! The Vicar greets typically enthusiastic congregation after another great sermon. You've got to *hand* it to him, haven't you?

Spot the mug! No it's not the Vicar! As ever, Tony is listening to what his parishioners have to say and thinking about it over a cup of tea. More T(ony) for all of us!

ST ALBION PARISH NEWS

30th June 2000

Hullo!

Well, the one thing you won't be hearing anything about from me this week is the football!

Let's face it, it's just a game. And not one I personally take any interest in. But to hear the way some people go on and on about it, you'd think it was a religion!

Surely people have got more important things to think about than whether the St Albion's team lost to a Belgian side last week solely because the silly Neville boy let everybody down by giving away a penalty in the last minute.

Of course, I was too busy preparing for the oecumenical conference in Portugal to watch the game myself, but from the moment the other side scored in the 20th minute I could see we were going to lose.

And you know, it's so easy to get these things out of proportion. Which is why a group of St Albion's supporters went and threw chairs through the window of Mr and Mrs Magritte's chocolate shop (Pralines Sont Nous) in the High Street.

I would like to offer an apology on behalf of our whole parish community to Mr and Mrs Rene Magritte for the mindless actions of a tiny and completely unrepresentative minority of our youth club members. And I can give them a solemn promise that this will not happen again since St Albion's are now, sadly, out of the Interparish 2000 competition.

So, enough of football! I'm not going to devote the whole of my letter to what is nothing more than a past-time, with its literal meaning of "passing the time".

And talking of "passing", I have to say that this was just one of the things which let us down so badly.

It was embarrassing for all of us who watched the game from start to finish to see just how badly our team was outplayed. Like it or not, a humiliation like this reflects badly on the whole parish and on its leadership, which means me.

Obviously, it is not my fault if the team loses. But, let's face it, if we had won, which is what we were all praying for at Evensong last Sunday, it would have made everyone feel better about themselves and the way the parish is going.

And, as for the hooligans, all I can say is that their disgraceful boorishness was even worse than the bad manners recently displayed by the so-called ladies of the St Albion's Women's Institute, many of whom, Mr Campbell tells me, are fully paid-up members of extremist right-wing groups like the Townswomen's Guild.

So, as we look back on all these distressing recent events, let us remember that football is not just a game. It is a microcosm of life itself (which is why I have always been so keen on it!). We all play our part, whether on the field itself or in the stands, singing those much-loved old hymns, "Here We Go" and "Que Sera, Sera".

Yours,

Tony

(in the number 10 shirt of life!)

✉ Parish Postbag

From Mrs Jay, Matron of the St Albion's People's Old Home (formerly Home For Distressed Gentlefolk)

Dear Vicar,

I am sick and tired of parishioners accusing me of lying about where I went to school. When I said I had been to the local grammar school, it was quite obvious that what I meant was that I attended the St Albion's High School for Young Ladies, where grammar played a central part in the English curriculum.

Yours faithfully,
Mrs Margaret Jay
(née Callaghan)

P.S. The Editor reserves the right not to print any letters disagreeing with the above, particularly if they come from deranged inmates of the old folks' home, like Mr Normo Tebbs.

✝ To Remember In Your Prayers

● Mr Roy Jenkins who has been a loyal friend of the Vicar's for many years, but who has now repaid the Vicar's kindness and hospitality with an unforgivable and uncharitable attack, accusing the Vicar of having "a second-rate mind".

Help Roy to cope with his increasing senility and, of course, his tragic problem of over-consumption of claret. May he learn to come to terms with his own failure to become Vicar and accept his increasing obscurity with good grace.

T.B., MA Oxon – a real degree, Roy!

Parish Notices

St Albion's Weightwatchers will be meeting in the Church Hall on Tuesdays. Mrs Jowell will be helping any ladies who are having problems putting on weight. The first meeting will focus on "Cakes and Puddings" and our future themes include "Our Friend The Potato", "Are You Getting Enough Sugar?" and "Trust In The Lard".

Fatsheets available from Mrs Jowly's website thin-no-more @churchhall.co.uk

Millennium Tent update
From Jean-Claude Gerbil, Grand Directeur de la Tente Millenniale

Bonjour!

Et un grand remercie à notre cher ami Monsieur Heseltine (Tarzan de la jungle, comme vous dites!). Il a dit que la Tente est la plus populaire attraction dans le whole monde! Et c'est vrai! La Tente a already attracté plus de visiteurs than

- *Le Monte D'Everest*
- *Le Wreck du Titanic*
- *Le North Pole*
- *Le Lost Kingdom De L'Atlantis*
- *La Lune.*

Pour example, regardez cette charte:

Nombre de visiteurs à la lune cette semaine: **0**
Nombre de visiteurs à la Tente: **1**

Eh voilà! Sorted! Comme les young people disent! J-C. G.

☠ **WARNING!** ☠

It has come to my notice that various younger and more impressionable members of our congregation have fallen under the spell of an undesirable American evangelist (Rev. Marvin O'Bushlicker, First Church of Christ The Free-Marketeer). Only those with no ideas and nothing in their heads (eg, Master Hague) would fall for this kind of nonsense. If young William is looking for a spiritual leader, perhaps I could direct him to a charismatic figure rather closer to home! T.B.

ST ALBION PARISH NEWS

14th July 2000

Hullo!

Or, at least, hullo to all those of you who understand the meaning of the word "loyalty"!

And inevitably that's my theme this week, after such a spectacular display of ingratitude and betrayal by one of our parishioners.

As you know, Mr Follett (or "Ken" as Cherie and I used to call him) was once one of the most trusted members of our parish inner circle. "The Vicarage Kitchen Cabinet" you might call it.

Ken and his wife Barbara were always available to give a helping hand with our parish fund-raising initiatives – such as giving prizes for the white elephant stall at the fête, collecting envelopes for restoring Mr Cook's organ and throwing big parties for the Vicar.

And why not? Let's be frank about this. Ken has done pretty well for himself, dashing off his little books. And without being disloyal – I think we can leave that to him! – we can all agree that they are badly-written potboilers which scarcely deserve to fetch 10p on the second-hand bookstall at the parish jumble sale. Still, Ken has made a pile of money out of his so-called literary activities, and here was a chance to give back to the community some of his ill-gotten gains!

It was a chance to make amends! After all, remember the young, rich man who asked Our Lord what he could do to be saved *(Gospel of St Lukre, 7.13)*? And the reply came, "Sell all that you have and give your money to Me."

Ken may have followed this advice for a while, but in the end the deadly sin of pride was too much for him.

Just because he was friends with the Vicar, he began to think he was someone really important in the life of the parish! He thought his *opinions* mattered, rather than his money!

To be honest, he became a bit of an embarrassment – which was why Cherie and I decided, for the good of the parish, that he and his equally embarrassing wife Barbara should no longer be invited to break *ciabatta* with us at our dinner parties!

I am sorry to say that, instead of just accepting that we didn't want to see him any more, or hear his silly views on parish business, or listen to his awful wife telling members of the PCC what colour ties to wear at evensong, Ken turned spiteful in a quite unforgiveable way.

The next thing we knew was that he was being quoted in the local paper, the St Albion Observer and Advertiser, attacking me for being "disloyal" and for being unpleasant about my colleagues behind their backs.

Perhaps it is time Ken was reminded of the most famous biblical story of all – the man who betrayed his leader after being a trusted disciple.

Ring any bells, Ken? I don't know whether there are any trees in your enormous garden, but Mr Campbell is sending you a suitable length of rope and I trust you'll know what to do with it!

Yours more in anger than in sorrow,

Tony

SOLE Team Leader of the Parish Project!

THE EDITOR WRITES:

In response to recent criticism that my personality has become too dominant in parish life, I want to make it clear that from now on I propose to take a back seat, and to refrain from making any comments at all on individual members of the PCC. For example, I shall not be putting it about that Mrs Mowlam's unfortunate personality problems stem from her love of the bottle. Nor will I be telling the regulars at the Britannia Arms that Mr Brown should be seeking psychiatric help as a matter of urgency. Nor under any circumstances will you find me whispering in people's ears over a game of darts at the Working Men's Club that Mr Prescott is an over-weight buffoon who dyes his hair and who can't even say the words "Good morning" in the right order. No, I understand the meaning of the word "loyalty", which is why, from now on, I will leave it to the Vicar to do his own dirty work!

Alastair Campbell, Editor

━━━━━ SALVE! ━━━━━

A warm welcome to my old friend John Birt who, even though he knows nothing about crime (apart from watching "The Bill"), has generously volunteered to give up a day a week to chair the Neighbourhood Watch Focus Group on 'Illegal Parking in Vicarage Crescent'. Thanks John – St Albion's needs men of your calibre in the Fight Against Crime.

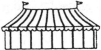

MILLENNIUM TENT UPDATE

by Jean-Claude Gerbil

Moi – je suis malade comme un parrot! Et no mistake! Le tent est un grand flop – mais ce n'est pas my fault! Oh non! Je will point le finger aux guilty men, quand le time comes – ie, when je suis sacked comme Madame Page, Monsieur – et tous les autres.

Mais, voici un few noms pour going on with: Monsieur Falconer: quel idiot! Monsieur Mandelson: un autre grand idiot! Et le Monsieur Big, le plus grand idiot de tout – Monsieur Tony

(This update has been cut for reasons of space. Mr Gerbil is very tired and has been recommended for a large salary increase and a life peerage. Alastair Campbell, Editor.)

?????????????? WHAT'S IN A NAME?

Have you ever noticed how people with the same name often share similar character traits?

For example, Bobby Moore and Bobby Charlton were both good footballers. Johann Bach and Johann Strauss both wrote nice tunes. And guess what! Ken Livingstone and Ken Follett are both treacherous, disloyal and deeply unpleasant human beings. Can you think of any others to add to the list?

??????????????

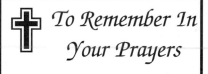

✝ To Remember In Your Prayers

…Mr Levy from the record shop in the High Street who is my special friend and advisor and who has been unfairly found out over his tax returns. Let his critics remember the words of our saver, "Render unto Caesar that which is Caesar's, unless it can be incorporated into the previous Tax Year!" *(Book of Levi the Profit, 3.15.)*

✝ Not To Remember In Your Prayers

…Mr Follett. T.B.

Special Edition of the
ST ALBION PARISH NEWS

21st July 2000

Reprinted In Full!

THE VICAR'S SERMON TO BRIGHTON'S
FIRST CHURCH OF HOT GOSPELLERS

The Vicar was due to preach on the subject of "Punishing the Yobs" but changed his mind at the last minute to "The Prodigal Son and the Need for Forgiveness"

Praise the Lord!

Brothers and sisters, I thank you all for your support during what has been a terrible week for me and my family. As the American poet Martin Luther Blackfellow put it so well, "Nobody knows the troubles I've seen." And it is at times like these that one looks forward to a really good holiday. And my thanks once again to Prince Fribi of Tuscany for lending me his Palazzo in Montepithonia.

(At this point, the Vicar appeared to be very tired and his thoughts began to ramble somewhat.)

I am sorry, brothers and sisters, I haven't been getting very much sleep lately due to my wife keeping me awake at night shouting "It's your turn" And that's only the new son. z-z-z-z-z.

(At this point, the Vicar fell asleep before being woken by Mr Campbell.)

All of you who are parents know how difficult it is when someone you love goes off the rails, begins to rebel against authority and gets drunk. I'm thinking of course of Mo Mowlam here and our prayers go out to her at this difficult time.

(At this point, Mr Campbell took Mr Blair home for a lie-down. The Choir then sung the anthem "Every Vicar's Worst Nightmare", Words and Music T. Blair.)

M. J-C GERBIL, GRAND CHEF DE LA MILLENNIUM TENTE

Attention, enfants de St Albion!

Regardez cet picture de moi très carefully! Vous êtes feeling sleepy n'est-ce-pas? Vous êtes drowsy... non?

Comptez a ten – un, deux, trois vous êtes relaxing? Quatre, cinq, six, êtes-vous totalement dans un trance hypnotiquue, le fameux "Trance de Gerbil"?

Maintenant. Quand vous wake-up vous will go immediatement à la tente Millennium.

Vous will have vraiment

"One exciting jour to remember"!

"L'experience d'un lifetime"!

"Un not boring time at all, regardless of what tout le monde dit"!

Alors, je snap my fingers – et voilà! Bienvenue à la tente!

© J-C. Gerbil, le Grand Mesmeriste de Disneyworld!

ST ALBION PARISH NEWS

28th July 2000

Hullo!

Or at least "hullo" to those of you who haven't already read a draft version of this letter in "leaked" form among your e-mails!

You know, it's not very nice, is it, to think that everything you do or say in the privacy of your own vicarage is liable to be broadcast all over the parish for everyone to sneer at?!

I wonder if the person who's doing this has ever stopped to think how much distress and suffering it causes? Not just to me (after all, it's my job to "turn the other cheek"), but to all those in the parish who have been working so hard and so long to achieve all the targets that the team-ministry has been aiming for over the past three years.

You all know what I'm referring to – the two leaked items of correspondence which in recent days have appeared on the front page of the St Albion's Messenger.

Firstly, there was my top-secret and totally private memo to the steering group of the PCC under the heading "Why Aren't You Getting My Message Across?"

And, secondly, there was the reply from Mr Gould, who runs our house-groups network, headed "Because You Haven't Got A Message, You Idiot".

Mr Gould is, of course, perfectly entitled to his views and to express them in his customary forthright manner. But, as the Vicar, I am sure you will all agree that I am equally entitled to ask Mr Gould to take a very long holiday somewhere where he cannot e-mail me with his thoughts, eg, the bottom of the sea!

But, you know the really sad thing about all the ridiculous fuss which has been made about these two trivial little parish memos is that it has diverted everyone's attention away from the real good news of the week!

I mean, of course, the fact that, after very carefully doing our sums, the parish is now in a position to give very substantial and generous sums of money to all sorts of local good causes, from our cottage hospital to St Albion's primary school.

This means that at long last we will be able to do all sorts of things you've been wanting us to do, but we haven't been able to, because Mr Brown, our Treasurer, has been so slow in geting on top of the figures. No offence, Gordon, you've been doing the best you can, but perhaps I should have been quicker to help you – only I've been rather busy lately, what with the lack of sleep and broken nights! You understand, Gordon! Or rather you don't, because for some reason you still haven't got married, let alone had children, which is odd for a person of 46. Not that I think so, Gordon, but you know what people are like, they will say "There's no smoke without fire" (*Proverbs*, 7.4).

Mr Brown has rightly been credited for being the one who had the chance to announce all our new spending plans. But let us not lose sight of whose money it is that Gordon is giving away. It's not his money, is it? It is the parish's money. And, as the vicar of this parish, the money could be said to be mine and mine alone!

And now, Cherie and I are taking a well-earned holiday in Tuscany with our old friend Prince Fribi. As usual, I am leaving Mr Prescott in charge of the day-to-day running of the parish. But if anything important crops up, Mr Campbell knows where to find me!

Arrivederci!

Toni

HURRY!HURRY!HURRY!

Copies of the **St Albion's Parish Annual Report** (with foreword by the Vicar) are still available from Tesco's, at the bargain price of £2.99 for 1000. If you want to find out what's really going on in the parish, read Mr Campbell's independent account of how well we have done this year! Remember, out of 177 promises, Tony and the team have managed to keep 178! Not bad, eh!

HURRY!HURRY!HURRY!

£ PARISH GIVING £

Where The Benefits Will Go

● New part-time music teacher (Tuesday mornings) for St Albion's Primary School
● New bus-stop outside vicarage with all-weather shelter
● Registered osteopath to visit cottage hospital (Fridays)
● Extension of parish bicycle lane network to include cemetery and youth club

---

Text of The Week

"They toil not, neither do they spin. Yet they remain very popular and get their message across!"

(Letter to the Philipgouldians).
I think there's a lesson for us all here! T.B.

Millennium Tent Update
Message from J-C Gerbil, Grand Supremo de Tente

Bonjour, mes amis!

Et j'ai très bonnes nouvelles!

Pour les school vacances, nous avons thought up beacoup de nouveaux attractions!

1. Continuous showing d'un video de la Pageant Centennaire pour la Queen Mother.

2. Exposition des mobile phones (merci à nos amis de Vodaphone).

3. Le Grand Morris-Dancing! Festival de dance folklorique d'Angleterre! Oubliez le Salsa! Maintenant, c'est les Morrismen de Hemel Hempstead. Admission totalement libre!

Ne soyez pas un sheep! (Merci à M. Saatchi pour cet brilliant slogan!)

J-C. G.

SAYONARA!

That's "hi!" in Japanese! And here's a snap of yours truly getting shirty(!) on behalf of the poor and needy in the Third World. At a big Ecumenical conference with all the other world spiritual leaders, we all agreed that something should be done about the poor! So that's good news for the starving! Now I'm off to a big lunch to celebrate our achievement!

Sayonara, which also means "Bye"!   T.B.

The "MILLENNIUM TAPESTRY", showing scenes of parish life through the ages, from 1997 to the present day, has finally been completed and is now on show in the Church Hall. Our thanks to all the ladies who spent so much time creating this masterpiece and to Mr Campbell for coming up with the prizewinning design!

ST ALBION PARISH NEWS

11th August 2000

Hullo!

Or should I say "Salve!", as I am writing to you this week from the wonderful olive groves of the Palazzo Splendido, the delightful little 200-bedroom villa which Cherie, I and the kids have been lucky enough to be lent by our very good friend Count Fribi.

Since we came out here, I have had a lot of time to reflect on some of the deeper moral challenges that confront us all in these confused times. And one of these, obviously, is the issue of my photograph.

I know everyone wants to take my picture, and that is perfectly understandable, considering how important I am! But there are times, surely, when all of us have the right not to have our picture taken!

And one such occasion was the recent christening of baby Leo which was a very private event to mark the occasion of our son's public welcome into the parish community.

And what happened? Even though we had specifically asked for everyone to respect our privacy, there the next morning on the front page of the St Albion's Clarion was a large photograph of yours truly posing for the camera with baby Leo.

At first, Cherie and I were deeply upset. She even suggested ringing up one of her friends who is a judge, to see if somebody could be put in prison!

Mr Campbell was so angry that he suggested that this year none of our holiday snaps should be published in the parish magazine, as a way of letting people know just how determined we are to keep out of the public eye!

But no! Wiser counsels (ie, mine) prevailed. Nothing is gained by being vindictive. As it says in the Good Book, "Turn the other cheek towards the camera" *(St Paul's Letter To The Paparazzionians).*

So that is why, when we arrived in Italy, I very reluctantly invited several hundred photographers to take whatever pictures they like, and Mr Campbell has said that he will publish the best of them to go alongside this letter!

But really we must move on to more serious matters. Goodness me, wouldn't it be a pretty silly waste of time if the only thing I managed to write about in this letter was people taking pictures of me and my family! Ciao!

Toni

Wedding Bells (At Last!)

*O*ur warmest congratulations to Gordon and Sarah for at last having the decency to tie the knot! I must admit most of us had long since given up hope that the day would ever come, especially when I had read their Banns 349 times! I suppose it is better late than never, and it was right of Gordon not to make a big song and dance about it as if it was a proper wedding. Incidentally, I know that a lot of you, bearing in mind how suddenly it all happened, will be thinking there was something rather fishy about their marriage. But, let me assure you that this wasn't the case! (At least not as far as I know!) T.B.

PS. I am sure that Gordon, being a thrifty Scot, would not wish parishioners to spend their hard-earned savings on giving him a wedding present. Cherie and I certainly won't!
PPS. Cherie and I were not at all offended at not being invited to Gordon's wedding, even though he is our next-door neighbour and a very old friend, and only has his job thanks to me! We were very busy anyway, that day, packing to go on holiday, and even if Gordon had invited us, we would probably have had to decline!

The Working Men's Club

A notice from Mr Prescott

"The club will be closed during August for essential refurbishment to be carried out at a cost of £100,000. The Secretary's office requires a new carpet in keeping with the status of the Working Men's Club as one of the most historic buildings in the parish (built 1965, snooker room extension added 1982). For anyone who is interested, the carpet is a hand-woven original Axminister showing a pair of Jaguars Rampant above the monogram 'JP' in Argent."

Good News!

A very warm welcome to young Ivan Massow, who has decided to join our congregation after, as he puts it, "seeing the light". Mr Massow's conversion is marvellous news, particularly since he is exactly the sort of person we want at St Albion's – ie, someone who has the courage to admit openly that he has a lot of money, and is not ashamed of it!
T.B.

Parish Postbag...

Dear Sir,
No one could accuse me of being prejudiced against any minority, but frankly it makes me sick to see the Vicar welcoming with open arms a self-confessed fox-hunter who admits hanging round in the woods with other men, waiting for
> *Yours sincerely*
> *Ken Livingstone, Dunnuthin,*
> *Newt Road.*

The Editor reserves the right to cut all letters from Mr Livingstone for reasons of personal dislike.

ST ALBION PARISH NEWS

25th August 2000

Hullo,

But a very short one this week because, hey, guess who's the writer in the family now?

Just as I was about to pen my thoughts to you from our holiday in distant Italy, Cherie walked in and I had a brilliant idea – which was to agree to her suggestion that she should write this week's message!

And why not? After all, we're a modern family. And if I help her by changing the nappies and holding little Leo whenever there are any photographers around, why shouldn't she do my job from time to time?

So, it's over to you Cherie! It's all yours!

Cherie Booth (the Vicar's wife) writes:

As you all know, I am an independent working woman in my own right. The fact that I have become a very successful lawyer has nothing whatever to do with the fact that I am married to the Vicar.

In fact, if anything, it is the other way around. I don't think I am giving away any secrets if I say that Tony has only got where he is today thanks to my support, advice and encouragement.

And, in view of the meagre size of a vicar's stipend, I can also tell you that if it wasn't for my contribution to the family budget, we would scarcely be able to come on our all expenses paid holiday to Italy!

That is why I am extremely angry at suggestions being made round the parish that I have used my position to "cash in" in my new legal practice.

Frankly, this is typical of the kind of sniping we have come to expect from a totally male-dominated culture, which in my own profession is so rampant that I sometimes think they are still living in the Middle Ages.

These same people have been saying behind my back that I have gone back to work far too soon after the birth of our son Leo.

But, frankly, in the modern world it is not my job to look after the baby night and day. I have more important things to do, which is why I expect Tony to play his full part.

And, I have to say, he has done a very good job, so far at least! And I hope that people in the parish will recognise this.

So, the next time they see Tony nodding off at a PCC meeting, or stumbling over his words in the pulpit, I hope they will make allowances. He has probably been up all night with Leo, so that I can get a good night's rest and go off to do a full day's work at the office to keep the show on the road!

And very soon I shall be even busier than usual, when the new human rights legislation comes into effect, which will create a huge amount of extra work for us lawyers, who are already pretty over-burdened as it is!

But the last thing I want to do is to use the Vicar's newsletter to go on about my professional concerns! So, let me end by simply reminding any parishioner who wants legal advice on human rights or anything else for that matter, that I can be contacted at the vicarage at any time (except nights of course!) or at my new office in Matrix House in the High Street.

Good sueing!

CHERIE BLAIR

Tony adds:

Great stuff, Cherie! I must let you write the newsletter more often! How refreshing for a change to have a woman's view on the big moral issues of our time. T.B.

Tony's Little Blessing

The Vicar relaxes on his well-earned holiday in France. But rest assured – he's still holding the baby.

ST ALBION'S COMPREHENSIVE

Mr Blunkett writes:

Yet again I must congratulate St Albion's pupils on their superb performance in scoring a record 102 percent of A Grades in our recent A Levels.

I am sure the Vicar's wife will be particularly pleased to know that for the first time the St Albion's girls did much better than the boys! I am sure there is a lesson for us all here, but I am not sure what it is! D.B.

Master Euan Blair

The Editor Writes:
I know the last thing the Vicar wants is for me to comment, but he has asked me to put on record his disapproval of the way people are continuing to comment about his young son, and in particular the so-called "incident" that never happened.

The Vicar says that he himself is "fair game" – so long of course that nothing detrimental is said. But his family are a "No-Go Area". And Cherie warns everyone that when the new European laws come into place, there will be a heavy price to pay by those who don't take these words to heart! A.C.

 ## Millennium Tent Update

J-C Gerbil writes:

Mesdames, messieurs! Plus de bonnes nouvelles au sujet du Tent Millenniaire!

Nous avons agreed avec notre bon ami M. Nomura de Tokyo qu'il will "take the tent off our hands" ce automne pour une somme "très raisonable" (3p).

Il a beaucoup de bonnes idées pour fair le tente profitable, et je serais le first in the queue pour voir qu'est-ce qu'il a come up with! Le Hypermarché de Tesco, peut-être?

Au revoir,
Jean-Claude Gerbil

PS. Oubliez-pas – il y a encore beaucoup de tickets pour vous et votre famille. See vous there!

PPS. Aussi, pour un jour seulement, Le Grand Festival de Pokémon. Achetez les cards et download Le Mu!

"Un Jour Incroyable"

A Message From Mr Prescott

As you know, I have been left holding the fort as per usual, while the Vicar and his lady enjoy one of their well-earned holidays in that posh foreign palace provided by one of their rich Italian friends.

I am sure we all hope they have had a good rest, which Tony particularly needs after all the trouble he has had looking after the baby.

I am sure Tony wouldn't want me to say this, but I have to say that I absolutely agree with what young Master Hague was saying the other day about paedophiles – ie, that they should be taken out and shot. Well spoken, lad!

And if it's your idea of fun to sink 14 pints of ale of an evening, you'd be welcome at the Working Men's Club any time! J.P.

ST ALBION PARISH NEWS

8th September 2000

Bonjour!

That's European for hullo!

And the good news is that Cherie and I are back from a wonderful holiday, ready to hit the ground running on all cylinders and with our batteries raring to go!

Doesn't it do us all good to get away for a few weeks, staying with generous friends and business contacts in agreeable villas all round the continent.

How small some of our worries can seem when we look at them from beside a swimming pool, or across a Tuscan olive grove!

Hey! I'll be frank. When I went away I was a little bit wound-up about those photos of me and baby Leo which had appeared in the St. Albion's Advertiser against my wishes. Even on holiday, I got pretty ratty, I can tell you, when I took the family to church and found a local photographer waiting outside with a bottle of wine and asking Euan to pose with it lying in the road!

But then I said to myself, "Look Tony, these people are only human, and they're only doing their job like the rest of us. They're bound to be interested in anything you or your family do, because you're the most talked-about English vicar anyone has ever seen!"

So I decided to take a leaf out of the good book, when it says, "Let not your wrath go down upon the Sun, no, nor upon the Mirror neither." (*Your 100 Best Proverbs*, Ch.7)

And that's when I resolved that I should learn to "forgive and forget" as our Lord put it (*Little Book Of Forgiving And Forgetting*, Ch.15 v.3) and to make a completely fresh start and to show that we really want to be friends with everyone working in the local media!

I put my thoughts on this into a chorus, which Mr. Campbell and I have recorded on a special tape for our popular local hospital radio service, "Get Well Soon FM". Here is how it goes:

> *"What a friend we have in Tony*
> *What a friend he is indeed,*
> *What a friend we have in Tony*
> *He's the guy who's born to lead."*
> (repeat)

© Words and music copyright A.R.P. Blair, with additional material by A. Campbell

Your friend,

Tony

✝ To Remember In Your Prayers

Mr.Branson (right), who has offered to take over the running of the Parish tombola from Mr. Camelot (entirely free of charge I may add, apart from his expenses, of course!) Let us pray that Mrs. Shovelton and her ladies come to a sensible decision on this one, when they have their steering committee meeting next week, and choose the right person for this very important job. Mr. Branson is a very old friend, but I would not of course for a moment wish to influence the good ladies by revealing that he is the man I have chosen for the job! T.B.

Cherie's Recipe For RICH SUMMER PUDDING

(held over from last issue)

Ingredients

Fruits of office, huge amounts of bread, bags of dough and plenty of gravy.

Directions

Mix well and add sweeteners to taste.
Soak until nicely rich.
Serves one.

Announcement

There will be a meeting of AAA (Albion Alcoholics Anonymous) in the Church Hall on Friday. Anyone who is prone to get drunk and start ranting about how useless the Vicar is should take advantage of this meeting. Cherie's father, Mr Booth (or "Booze" as he is known in the family!), would be well advised to attend or he might find himself in prison. T.B.

Seasonal Offer

Ideal Gifts For the Festive Winter Season (formerly Christmas)

THE VICAR MUG COLLECTION

specially made for St Albion's by Photomug Ltd., Mowlam, Staffs

The "Tea Blair" Mug £25.99

The "Anyone for Cherie?" Mug £12.99

The "Whole Family" Mug £7.99 (as seen on TV)

The "Little Leo Beaker" Mug £59.99

The "Euan Blair Pint" Mug £5.99

All proceeds to the Parish Fighting Fund

From Mr Blunkett, Chairman of Governors at the St Albions Secondary School.

600 words that all pupils will be expected to spell

Everyone	And
Thinks	Does
The	A
Vicar	Terrific
Is	Job
Marvellous	Here

The rest of the words can be obtained on request from Mr Campbell.

Parish Postbag

From Canon D. Owen

Dear Sir,

I would like to put on record once and for all that all the vicar's ideas about his so-called "Third Way" etc. were all taken from me. It was me who thought it all up as long ago as

> *Yours faithfully,*
> *D. Owen (Doctor of Divinity),*
> *London SDP NBG*

From Mr. Woy Jenkins (transcribed from the vicarage answering machine by Mr. Campbell)

I was vewy, vewy, vewy distwessed to learn that my far-weaching pwoposals for wadical weform of the pwocedures for elections to the Pawochial Church Council, involving a gweat measure of pwoportional repwesentation have been most wudely wejected. For thwee years I have worked night and day on wesearching this pwoject, for no more weward than the occasional cwate of clawet. Yet now I discover that all labours are in vain and to be thwown into the wubbish as if they were no more than

> *Yours sincerely,*
> *Woy Jenkins,*
> *Oxford Road*

The Editor reserves the right to cut all letters from former members of the so-called St. Albion's Gang of Four for obvious reasons.

Parish Appraisement Form
Your chance to tell us how the parish is doing!

Just fill in the boxes below, so that YOUR VOICE can be heard!

1. Having read this book, would you describe it as
   - ☐ A very good book
   - ☐ An outstanding book
   - ☐ The best book you've ever read?

2. Would you say that the Vicar, the Rev. A.R.P. Blair
   - ☐ Has done a great job
   - ☐ Has done a really fantastic job
   - ☐ Is the best vicar we've ever had?

3. Would you say that, since the Rev. A.R.P. Blair became Vicar, the well-being of the parish
   - ☐ Has improved 100%
   - ☐ Has improved 200%
   - ☐ Is the best parish we've ever had?

...and, finally, What Do *You* Think?
The Vicar always values any comments from parishioners on how the running of the parish could be improved.

Here is your opportunity to put your suggestions direct to Tony (make sure to add your name and full address).

My suggestion to Tony is. . . . .

Just tear out this form and send it asap to:
The Vicarage Media Monitoring Unit, Room 308,
The Vicarage *(marked "Attention Mr Gould")*.